HOW TO BE A MAN

HOW TO BE A LADY

HARVEY NEWCOMB

HOW TO BE A MAN
HOW TO BE A LADY

A book for boys and girls, containing
useful hints on the formation of character

Walter Publications

ISBN 978-1-943939-81-7

PUBLISHER'S PREFACE

This book contains two works by the New England clergyman and writer Harvey Newcomb. These two works, titled *How to be a man* and *How to be a lady*, were published simultaneously and were written for boys and girls respectively. Since most of the text in the two works is identical, they are here brought together into one volume. To distinguish the text of the two works, chapters and sections taken from the book for boys are marked with the ornament ℘ ; they are followed by the corresponding sections from the book for girls, marked with ℘ .

The section titles that appear in this edition are not in the original books' tables of contents, and they do not occur in the text itself. They are partly based on the headers at the top of each page in the original. Their presence in the text and contents is intended to help in reading and reference.

HOW TO BE A MAN

A book for boys, containing useful hints
on the formation of character

by

HARVEY NEWCOMB,

Author of the "Young Lady's Guide," etc.

❦ PREFACE

"Who reads a preface?" Many do not, but jump at once into the middle of a book. But it is well to know something about a book, before reading it; and who so likely to give you information respecting the contents of a book as the Author himself? I wish to see the youth of my country come forward upon the stage of life, models of excellence, with characters formed for the times in which they are to act. How much influence my book may have, in securing such a result, I cannot tell; but my design in writing it has been, to contribute something toward forming the character of some of those who are to be our future electors, legislators, governors, judges, ministers, lawyers, and physicians – after the best model; and, from the kind reception of my former attempts to benefit American youth, I trust they will give a candid hearing to the few hints contained in the following pages. It is intended for boys – or, if you please, for *young gentlemen* – in early youth, from eight or ten to fifteen or sixteen years of age. It covers substantially the same ground occupied by a work for girls issued simultaneously with it; and some of the chapters are identical in the two books, while others are entirely different, and some partially so. It is the hope of the Author, that everyone who reads it, will strive to *be a man*, in the highest sense of the term.

JANUARY, 1847

HOW TO BE A LADY

A book for girls, containing useful hints
on the formation of character

by

HARVEY NEWCOMB,

Author of the "Young Lady's Guide," etc.

❧ PREFACE

"Preface! I never read a preface, it's *so prosy*," said a bright-eyed, sprightly little girl; "I want to get at the story." Her object in reading was *to be amused*. If she had desired to be benefited by what she read, she would have perused the Author's preface, in order to understand why he wrote the book. The "Young Lady's Guide" was intended for a class of females, who have attained some degree of maturity of character, and who are supposed already to have entered upon a religious life. The success of that work has led the Author, for several years, to contemplate the preparation of another, for a younger class of females. Having daughters of his own, and having been many years employed in writing for the young, he hopes to be able to offer some good advice, in the following pages, for girls or misses, between the ages of eight and fifteen. His object is, to assist them in forming their characters upon the best model; that they may become well-bred, intelligent, refined, and good; and then they will be LADIES, in the highest sense. This book covers substantially the same ground occupied by another work for boys, issued simultaneously with it. Some parts of both are identical; while other parts are entirely different. If it shall be the means of benefiting one immortal mind, the Author will be abundantly rewarded.

JANUARY, 1847.

CONTENTS

CHAPTER 1

ON CHILDHOOD & YOUTH

The great elm

In one sense, very young persons are apt to think too much of themselves – in another, not enough. When they think they know more than their parents and teachers, or other elderly people, and so set up to be *bold* and *smart*, then they think too much of themselves. It used to be said, when I was a boy, that "Young folks *think* old folks are fools; but old folks *know* young folks are fools." Although I would be very far indeed from calling you *fools*, because you have already acquired much knowledge, and have the capacity for acquiring much more, yet, with reference to such knowledge as is acquired by *experience*, and in comparison with *what there is to be known*, there is "more truth than poetry," in the old adage. But, when young people suppose it is of no consequence what they do, or how they behave, *because they are young*, then they do not think enough of themselves. Should you see a man riding with a little stick for a whip, you would not think his stick worth your notice at all; but the biggest tree that ever I saw grew from a little willow stick that a man rode home with, and then planted in his garden. You have sat under the beautiful shade of a great elm tree; and when you have looked upon its tall, majestic trunk, and its great and strong branches, with their ten thousand little limbs waving gracefully before the wind, you have been filled with admiration and delight. "What a mighty tree!" you say; "I wonder how long it has been growing." But the seed of that tree, when it was planted, many years ago, was no bigger than a mustard seed; and if you had seen the little tiny sprout that your grandfather was tying up with so much care, when it was a few years old, you would have wondered that a man should think so much of such an insignificant twig. But, if he had let it grow up as it began, without any care, it never would have been the stately tree it is now. That was the most important period in its life, when it was a little twig. It began to lean over, and grow crooked and ugly. If it had not been trained up then, it would have continued to grow worse and worse; and, after it had grown to be a tree, it could not have been straightened at all. Now, you are, in some respects, like this little twig. You, too, have just begun to be; and now your character is pliable, like the young tree. But, unlike it, your being is to have no end. Instead of growing a few hundred years, like a great tree, you are to live forever. And everything that you do now must have an influence in forming your character for your whole being. In this latter sense, you cannot think too much of yourself; for you are the *germ* of an immortal being.

Little things

Did you ever stand by the shore of a placid lake or pond, in a calm, sunny day, and throw a little stone into its smooth, silvery waters? Did you observe how, first, a little ripple was formed around the place where it struck, and this was followed by a wave, and then, beyond, another, and another, till the whole surface of the water was disturbed? It was a very little thing that you did; and yet it agitated a great body of water. So it is with childhood and youth; the most insignificant action you perform, in its influence upon your character, will reach through the whole period of your existence.

✄ Manliness

It will not do for you to say, "It is no matter how I behave now; I shall do differently when I am a man." "But would you have a little boy act like a man?" Not exactly. I would not have him affect the man, and appear as though he thought himself a full-grown gentleman. I would not have him imitate the *toad*, which undertook to swell to the size of an *ox*, and in the operation burst open. But, I would have him *manly* in his childishness. I would have him courageous, to meet difficulties, noble and generous in his feelings and actions, and courteous in his manners, always, in all companies, and in all places, behaving in a manner becoming a person of his age. A well-bred boy, who knows what is becoming and proper, and carries it out in his behavior, is already a *gentleman*. But the mischievous, rude, unmannerly lad, who pays no regard to propriety of conduct, will never be a gentleman. And a boy who has the courage to face difficulties, and the energy and perseverance to accomplish what he undertakes, is already *a man*; while the indolent, cowardly, *"I can't"* boy, will *never be a man*. It is my desire, in this book, to lead you to the formation of a solid, energetic, manly character, combined with true gentility of manners; and then you will be both a *man* and a *gentleman*.

✄ Being ladylike

It will not do for you to say, "It is no matter how I behave now; I shall do differently when I am a lady." What you are while you are a girl, you will be when you become a woman. "But, would you have a little girl act like a woman?" Not precisely. But I would have her act *like a lady*. Not to put on airs – not to put herself forward, and take the place of a woman before she is big enough to fill it – not to feel above labor, and despise those who perform it – not to look down with scorn upon everything that is common – not to treat with contempt those who cannot dress as well as herself, or who have not seen so much of *style and fashion*. Those who behave so are *pseudo-ladies*. A *true lady* would despise such meanness. To *be a lady*, one must behave always with propriety; and be civil, courteous, and kind, to all. To treat any human being with rudeness, would show a want of breeding of which no *lady* would be guilty. But the romping, roisterous miss, who pays no regard to propriety of conduct, will never be a lady. You will not, however, misunderstand me. Do not suppose that I would have you dull and mopish, never manifesting any gaiety of spirit or playfulness of conduct; but, in all these things, I would have you behave with strict regard to propriety.

The fairy world

Very young persons sometimes live in an *ideal world*. What they imagine in their plays seems real. They have a little fairy world in their minds, in which they live more, and take greater delight, than they do in what is real and true. To this I do not object, within certain bounds; but often it becomes a *passion*, so that they lose all relish for sober, everyday life. For such creatures of fancy, real life is too dull, and what concerns realities, too grave. Perhaps they will not like my book, because it treats of things true and real. But I beg them to consider that, through the whole of their being, they are to be concerned chiefly with *realities*; and therefore, to do them substantial good, we must speak to them of things real, and not of those airy things that belong to the fairy land. But real things are, truly, more interesting than the creations of fancy. The things of fancy interest you more only because they appear new and less common. A person who has always lived in the country, and is used to sitting under the wide-spreading, shady tree, would be more pleased with the *picture* of a tree than with a *tree itself*. But one brought up in the city would cast away the picture, and hasten to enjoy the cool shade of the beautiful tree. A castle in the air may please the fancy; but you want a *real house* to live in.

CHAPTER 2

NATURE & OBJECTS OF EDUCATION

Formation of character

Perhaps some of my readers, when they see the title of this chapter, will think only of confinement in school, of books, and of hard study, and so be inclined to pass over it, as a dry subject, which they have so much to do with, every day, that they have no wish to think of it in a moment of relaxation. But I beg them to stop a minute, and not throw me away, among the old schoolbooks, till they have heard me through. I assure them that I use the term *education* in a far different sense. I think it means much more than going to school and studying books. This is only a small part of education. Mr. Walker defines education, *"The formation of manners in youth."* But this is a very imperfect definition; and I am afraid there may be found some who would even doubt whether education has anything to do with manners. Mr. Webster gives a better definition: "Education comprehends all that series of instruction and discipline which is intended to enlighten the understanding, correct the temper, and form the manners and habits of youth, and fit them for usefulness in their future stations" – all, in fact, that is necessary to make a *man* or a *woman* – a *gentleman* or a *lady*.

The original root, from which the word *education* is derived, means to *lead out*, to *conduct*, to *form*, to *fashion*, to *beat out*, to *forge*. It was used with reference to the forging of an instrument out of a piece of metal, or the chiseling of a statue out of a block of marble. This furnishes a good illustration of my ideas of *education*. It is a process by which a character is formed out of rude or unwrought materials. It is not confined to mere school learning. A person may be very *learned*, and yet not half *educated*. There are many steps in the process. The ore must first be dug up by the miner; then smelted at the furnace, and the metal separated from the dross; then wrought into bars at the foundry; afterwards forged by the smith; and then, finally, polished by the finisher. The marble must first be quarried, or blasted out of the ledge; then cut into blocks; then transported; then wrought with the hammer and chisel; and finally, polished. This gives a good idea of education. It is not merely what is done to form the character in *school*; but it comprises all the influences which are exerted upon the young, in training them up and forming their characters. Education begins in the *family*. It is carried forward in the *school*. It is affected, for good or for evil, by the influence of public worship, lectures, books, amusements, scenery, companions, etc. In all places and circumstances, something is doing towards the formation of character.

Self-education

Yet there is one important respect in which *education*, or *the formation of character*, differs essentially from the process described in this illustration. The block of marble, or the piece of metal, is *passive*; the whole process is performed upon it by another. But no person can be educated in this way; everyone that is educated must be *active*. You may be drilled through all the schools, and have every advantage at home and in society; and yet, without your own active cooperation, you can never be educated. But, if you are determined to be educated, you will turn everything to some account. Everything will be a school to you; for you will make contributions to your stock of knowledge from every object you see; and by seeking to act discreetly, wisely, and correctly, in every place, you will be constantly forming good habits. Like the little busy bee, you will suck honey from every flower. You will commune with your own heart upon your bed, and exercise your powers of thought in useful meditation. You will converse with God in your secret place, and seek wisdom of Him who has promised to give liberally to those that ask. In company, you will be more ready to hear than to speak; and you will never meet with any so ignorant but you may learn from them some useful lessons. You will exercise your mind upon every person and object you meet. You will study philosophy in the fields, by the brooks, on the hills, in the valleys, and upon the broad canopy of heaven. It has been well observed, that the difference between a wise man and a fool is, that one goes through the world with his eyes wide open, while the other keeps them shut.

Footprints

You will perceive, then, that your education is continually going on, whether you think of it or not. Your character is constantly forming. It is your business to keep out of the way of bad influences, and submit yourself to the moulding of the good. Keep in mind the great truth that you are forming a character for eternity. Some years ago, there were found on the banks of the Mississippi River the tracks of a human being, deeply imprinted in the solid rock. These tracks were made in the soft clay, which in time became hardened, and formed into stone; now the impression is immovable. You now resemble this soft clay. Everything with which you come in contact makes an impression. But, as you grow older, your character acquires solidity, and is less and less affected by these influences, till at length it will be like the hard stone, and the impressions made upon you at this season will become confirmed habits.

All the impressions made upon your character ought to be such as will not need to be removed. Washington Allston, the great painter, had been a long time at work on a most magnificent painting. He had nearly completed it, when his keen eye discovered some defects in a portion of the piece. He hastily drew his rough brush over that portion of the picture, intending to paint it anew. But in the midst of his plans, death seized him, and his painting remains, just as he left it. No other person can carry out the conception that was in his mind. If you allow wrong impressions to be made upon your forming character, death may meet you with his stern mandate, and fix them forever, as immovable as it left the rough print of the coarse brush upon Allston's canvas.

CHAPTER 3

PIETY, AS THE SPRING OF ACTION, AND REGULATOR OF THE SOUL

The watch

A watch, to one who had never seen such a piece of mechanism before, would be a great wonder. It is an object of much curiosity to the natives of savage and barbarous tribes, visited by the missionaries. It seems to speak and move, as though instinct with life. I have read, somewhere, of a poor savage, who, seeing a white man's watch lying on the ground, and hearing it tick, supposed it to be some venomous reptile, and, with a stone, dashed it in pieces. A watch is an object of no less wonder to a child. Children are full of curiosity, as my readers well know. They wish to examine everything they see – to take it in pieces, and see how it is made. I dare say my readers remember the time when they sat on their father's knee, and modestly requested him to show them the little wheels of his watch.

If I could sit down with my young friends, and take my watch in pieces, I would teach them a useful lesson. I would show them how a watch resembles a human being. There is the *case*, which may be taken off, and put by itself, and still the watch will go as well as ever. In this respect, it is like the human body. Death separates it from the soul, and yet the soul remains, with all its active powers. It still lives. The inside of the watch, too, resembles the soul. It has a great many different parts, all working together in harmony – a great many wheels, all moving in concert. So the soul has a great many different powers or faculties, all designed to operate in concert with each other, as the *understanding*, the *judgment*, the *conscience*, the *will*, the *affections*, the *memory*, the *passions*, *desires*, etc.; and each one of these has a part to act, as important for the man, as the several wheels and springs of the watch. If every part of the watch is in order, and in its proper place, it will keep exact time; but, if one wheel gets disordered, it will derange the whole. The secret power that moves the watch is unperceived. If you examine, you will see a large wheel, with a smooth surface, round which is wound a long chain, attached to another wheel, with ridges for the chain to run upon. Inside of the first-named wheel is the *mainspring*, which, by means of the chain, moves the whole machinery. The WILL is the mainspring of the soul. By a mysterious, invisible chain, it holds all the powers of the soul and body at its command. Not only the operations of the mind, but the motions of the body are controlled by the will.

The balance wheel

But, if there were no check upon the mainspring of the watch, it would not give the time of day. It would set all the wheels in rapid motion, and in a few moments the watch would run down. To prevent this, there is a *balance wheel*, which turns backwards and forwards, by means of a fine spring, called the *hairspring*, and so keeps the whole machinery in a regular motion. To this is attached a little lever, called the *regulator*, which, by a gentle touch, works on this delicate spring, so as to move the balance wheel faster or slower, as the case may be, to make the movement exact and regular.

Now, if there were no checks on the will, it would run on impetuously in its course, without regard to consequences. And this we often see in persons called *willful, self-willed, headstrong*. Children are often so; if let alone, their stubborn will would lead them to rush on headlong to their own destruction. Without meaning to be very accurate in these illustrations, I shall call *judgment* the *balance wheel*. This is the faculty which perceives, compares, and decides, keeps the mind balanced, and prevents its running to extremes either way.

The regulator

The *hairspring* and *regulator* of the watch I shall compare with *conscience*. A very slight touch of the regulator moves the hairspring, and gives a quicker or a slower motion to the balance wheel. But, if the watch is out of order, oftentimes the movement of the regulator has no effect upon it. So, when the soul is *in order*, a very slight touch of conscience will affect the judgment and regulate the will. But often, the soul is so much *out of order*, that conscience will have no effect upon it.

The spring of action

But who touches the regulator of the watch? There is nothing in the watch itself to do this. The power that moves the regulator *is applied to it*. So, the conscience is moved. The *Word of God* enlightens the conscience, and the *Spirit of God* applies the word. And this brings me to the point which I had in my mind when I began this chapter. What a poor thing a watch is, when it is out of order. It is of no use. A watch is made to keep the time of day; but, when

it is out of order, it will keep no time. Or, if it is in order, and yet
not regulated, it will not keep the right time.

Now until the heart is changed by the grace of God, the *soul is
out of order*. It does not answer the purpose for which it was made.
The *will* is wrong; the *judgment* is wrong; the *conscience* is wrong.
And, whatever cultivation may be bestowed upon the mind, it will
not act aright. In the very beginning, then, you want *piety*, as the
mainspring of action, and the *regulator* of the soul. Without this,
you are not prepared to begin anything aright. Indeed, without it,
you have no sufficient motive to action. You seem to be toiling and
laboring and wearying yourself for nothing. But *piety towards God*
gives a new impulse to the mind. When you set out to improve
your mind, if you have no piety, the object to be gained by it is very
small. It can secure to you no more than, perhaps, a little additional
enjoyment, for the brief space you are to continue in this world.
But piety opens to you a wide field of usefulness in this life, and
the prospect of going forward in the improvement of your mind
as long as eternity endures. It must, therefore, give a new spring
and vigor to all the faculties of the soul. It does more. It *regulates*
the powers of the mind, and the affections of the heart, and gives
a right direction to them all.

I would persuade you, then, as the first and great thing, to *seek
God*. Remember what Christ has said – "Seek ye first the kingdom   Matt. 6:33
of God and his righteousness, and all these things shall be added
unto you." Here is the promise that you shall have all else that is
needful, if you seek God first. Yield your heart to him, and have
his kingdom set up there. Let him rule in your heart, and devote
yourself to his service, and he will supply all your need. This, also,
will give a right direction to all your faculties, and lay a good foundation of character. But, without it, you will be like a watch with-

out a balance wheel or a regulator; you will be fit neither for this life nor that which is to come. And, it is of the utmost importance that you should become pious now, while you are young. If you would form a good character, you must have a good foundation laid at the beginning. Nothing but this can make a good foundation. All your habits ought to be formed and settled upon religious principles. Religious motives should enter into all your efforts to improve your mind and cultivate your affections. And, should you neglect religion now, and afterwards, by the grace of God, be led to devote yourself to him, you will find it hard and difficult to overcome the wrong habits of mind and conduct which you will have formed.

Piety, then, is the first thing to be considered, in the *formation of character*. And remember, also, that you are forming character *for eternity*; and that your whole being, through a never ending existence, is to be affected by the character which you form now in your childhood and youth. If you lay the foundation of your character now in the love and fear of God, it will rise higher and higher, in excellence, beauty, and loveliness, for ever and ever. But if you lay the foundation in selfishness and sin, and build accordingly, it will forever be sinking lower in degradation and deeper in wretchedness.

CHAPTER 4

FILIAL PIETY

Duty toward parents

Next to your duty to God comes your duty to your *parents*; and you can never form an excellent, amiable, and lovely character, unless the foundation of it is laid in *filial piety*, as well as in piety towards God. Solomon says to the young, "Hear the instruction of Prov. 1:8–9 thy father, and forsake not the law of thy mother; for they shall be an ornament of grace unto thy head, and chains about thy neck." Nothing will make you appear so lovely in the eyes of others as a dutiful behavior towards your parents; and nothing will make you appear so unamiable and unlovely as a disrespectful, disobedient carriage towards them. No ornament sits so gracefully upon youth as filial piety; no outward adorning can compare with it.

Gratitude

Filial piety calls into exercise feelings towards your parents, similar to those which piety towards God calls into exercise towards him; such as esteem and veneration of his character, love to his person, confidence in his word, submission to his authority, and penitence for offences against him. When the heart is habituated to the exercise of these feelings towards parents, it is prepared the more readily to exercise them towards God. The promises which God has made to those who honor their parents, and his threatenings against those who dishonor them, are similar to those which he has made respecting honor and obedience to himself. You owe it, therefore, to God, to exercise filial piety, because he has required it, and because it is one of the means he employs to cultivate piety towards himself. *Gratitude*, also, should lead to filial piety, as well as to piety towards God; for what God is to man, only in a lower sense, the parent is to his child. Your parents are, under God, the authors of your being. The greater part of parents' lives is spent in rearing, supporting, and educating their children. For this they wear out their strength in anxious care and toil; they watch beside the bed of their children when they are sick, with tender solicitude and sleepless vigilance; they labor to provide for them. But good parents are, most of all, anxious that their children should grow up intelligent and virtuous, pious and happy. There is no being but God to whom children are so much indebted as to a faithful parent; and almost all the blessings that God bestows upon them come through their parents.

Habit of submission

Filial piety has great influence on future character. One who has never been in the habit of submitting to others, will always be headstrong and self-willed; and such a character nobody loves. You cannot always do as you please; and, if such is your disposition, you will always be unhappy when your will is crossed. You will be unwilling to submit to necessary restraints, and this will irritate, and keep you in misery; for you will never see the time in your life when you will be so entirely independent of others that you can have your own way in everything. Even the king on his throne cannot do this. But, if you have always been in the habit of submitting to your parents, these necessary restraints will be no burden. If, then, you would be respected, beloved, and happy, when you grow up and take your place in society, you must *honor your parents*. Cultivate the habit of submission to their authority; of respectful attention to their instructions; and of affection and reverence to their persons. These are the habits that will make you respected, beloved, and happy. But as God has joined a curse to parental impiety, so he makes it punish itself. And thus you will find that it is generally followed with the most dreadful consequences. Of this I might give many painful examples; but the narratives would swell my book to an immoderate size.

~

The whole duty of children to parents, is expressed by God himself in one word – HONOR. This word is chosen, with great felicity, to express all the various duties of children toward their parents. There is a great deal of meaning in this little word, *honor*.

Feelings toward parents

Do you ask, *"How shall I honor my parents?"* In the first place, you must honor them *in your heart*, by loving and reverencing them, and by cultivating a submissive, obedient disposition. It is not honoring your parents, to indulge an unsubmissive, turbulent spirit. To be angry with your parents, and to feel that their lawful commands are hard or unreasonable, is dishonoring them. The authority which God has given your parents over you is for your good, that they may restrain you from evil and hurtful practices, and require you to do what will be, in the end, for your benefit. When they restrain you, or require you to do what is not pleasing to you, they have a regard to your best interests. To be impatient of restraint, and to indulge hard feelings toward them, is doing them great dishonor. If you could read the hearts of your parents, and see what a struggle it costs them to interfere with your inclinations, you would feel differently. But these rebellious feelings of yours are not only against your parents, but against God, who gave them this authority over you.

Honoring parents in word

Children also honor or dishonor their parents by their *words*. You honor them, by addressing them in respectful language, and in a tone of voice indicating reverence and submission, giving them those titles that belong to their superior station. An example of this we have in the answer of Samuel to what he supposed the call of Eli – "Here am I," – a form of speech used by servants to their masters, and implying attention to what was said, and a readiness to execute what was commanded. But parents are dishonored, when their children answer them gruffly, or speak in a sharp, positive, angry, or self-important tone; or when they neglect to accompany their address with the usual titles of respect, but speak out bluntly, *"Yes,"* or *"No."* This shows the state of the heart. And I think the reason why it is so difficult, in these days, to teach children to say, "Yes, sir," "No, ma'am," etc., is, that they do not feel in their hearts the respect which these terms imply. You will perceive, by this remark, that I have no respect for the notion which prevails, in some quarters, that these expressions are not genteel.

1 Sam. 3

Children likewise dishonor their parents, when they answer back, and argue against their commands, or excuse themselves for not obeying. It is as much as to say, they are wiser than their parents – which is doing them a great dishonor. To speak to them in disrespectful, reproachful, or passionate language, or to speak of them or their authority in such language to others, is also a great offence against their honor. Under the law of Moses, God punished this offence in the same manner that he did blasphemy against himself: "He that curseth his father or his mother shall surely be put to death." This shows what a great offence it is in his sight. Ex. 21:17

Attention to instruction

Another way in which you honor your parents is, by giving respectful attention to their instruction and counsels. God has committed your instruction and training to them; and when they teach or advise you according to the Scripture, their instructions are the voice of God to you. If you despise their instruction, you cast contempt upon God, who speaks through them, and who says, "My son, hear Prov. 1:8 the instruction of thy father, and forsake not the law of thy mother." It is very natural for children to wish to follow their own inclinations. The impetuosity of youth would hurry them on, heedlessly, in the high road to ruin. And, often, they despise the wholesome instruction and advice of their parents, as only designed to interfere with their pleasures, and abridge their enjoyments; while, in truth, their parents look beyond *mere* pleasure, to that which is of greater importance. They look upon these things in the light which age and experience has given them. If you were going to a strange place, in a way with which you were not acquainted, and should meet one that had been that way before, you would put confidence in what he should tell you of the way, and follow his directions. Your parents have passed through the period of life on which you are now entering, and they know the way. You will do well to confide in them, and abide by their instructions. If you neglect to do so, you will be sure to get into difficulty. The path of life is beset, on every side, with bypaths, leading astray; and these bypaths are full of snares and pitfalls, to catch the unwary, and plunge them into ruin. Your parents have become acquainted with these ways, and know their dangers. If they are good people, and understand their duty to you, they will warn you against them; and it will be the height of folly for you to disregard their warnings. Multitudes, by doing so, have rushed heedlessly on to ruin.

Obedience

You must honor your parents, also, by a *prompt and cheerful obedience* to their lawful commands. I say *lawful*, because no one ought to obey a command to do what is positively wrong. If a wicked parent should command his child to break the Sabbath, to lie, or to steal, or to break any of God's commands, it would be the child's duty to refuse, and meekly submit to the punishment which the parent might inflict. It is not often that such things happen among us; but our missionaries in Constantinople have related two instances that are in point. Two little Armenian girls had learned to read, and obtained from the missionaries some ideas of Christian morality. A person knocked ai the door of their house, and their father, not wishing to see him, told one of them to go and tell the person that he was *not at home*. "That would be telling a lie," said the daughter. "What then?" said the father; "it is a very little thing. You have only to say that I am not at home." "But, father," she replied, "the Bible says it is wicked to tell lies, and I cannot tell a lie." He was angry, and called his other daughter, and told her to go. She replied, "Father, I cannot, for it is wicked to lie." These children did right in refusing to obey such a command. But in no other case, except when told to do what is wrong, will a child be justified in refusing to obey.

Obedience must be *prompt* and *cheerful*. Your parents are not honored, when obedience is delayed to suit your convenience; nor when you *answer back*, or try to *reason against* your parents' commands, or plead for delay, that you may first finish your own work. A parent who is honored will never have to repeat the same command. Some children are bent on having their own way, and attempt to carry their point by showing their parents that their way is best; which is the same as saying to them that they are more ignorant than their children. Neither is *sullen obedience* honoring your parents. Some children, who dare not disobey their parents, will go about doing what is required of them with great reluctance, with perhaps a sullen expression of the countenance, a flirt, an angry step, or a slam of the door, or some other show of passion. Such conduct is a grief to parents, and an offence against God, who will not count that as obedience, which is not done cheerfully. But if you truly honor your parents from the heart, you will not wait for their *commands*. You will be always ready to obey the slightest intimation of their wishes. It is a great grief to a parent, when, out of respect to his child's feelings, he has expressed his *wish*, to be obliged to add his *command*, before the thing will be done. But filial piety never appears so amiable and lovely as when it anticipates the wishes of parents, and supersedes the necessity of expressing those wishes in advice or commands.

A right heart

If you honor your parents in your heart, you will pay an equal regard to their counsels and commands, whether they are present or absent. If you cast off their authority as soon as you are out of their sight, you greatly dishonor them. Such conduct shows that you do not honor them at all in your heart, but obey them only when you cannot disobey without suffering for it. But if you keep their authority always present with you, then you will do them great honor; for you show that they have succeeded in fixing in your heart a deep-seated principle of reverence and affection for them. If you truly honor your parents *in your heart,* you will obey them as well when they are absent as present. The parents' authority and honor are always present with the good child.

Children, likewise, honor or dishonor their parents in their *general behavior.* If they are rude and uncivil, they reflect dishonor upon their parents; for people say, they have not been trained and instructed at home. But when their behavior is respectful, correct, pure, and amiable, it reflects honor upon the parents. People will judge of the character of your parents by your behavior. Are you willing to hear your parents reproachfully spoken of? No, your cheek would glow with indignation at the person who should speak ill of your father or your mother. But you speak evil of them, in your conduct, every time you do anything that reflects dishonor upon them in the eyes of others. The blame of your conduct will be thrown back upon your parents.

But the true way to honor your parents, at all times and in all circumstances, is, to have your heart right with God. If you have true piety of heart toward God, you will show piety toward your parents; for you will regard the authority of his commandment, and delight in doing what will please him. The fear of God, dwelling in your heart, will lead you to reverence all his commands, and none more continually and conscientiously than the one which requires you to honor your parents. Everything that you do for Eph. 6:6–7 them will be done, "not with eyeservice, as menpleasers, but with good will, doing service as to God, and not to man."

✤ Feeling big

Boys of a certain age are frequently disposed to show their importance, by assuming to be wiser than their parents. They call in question the wisdom of their parents' directions, and seek, in every possible way, to set up their own will. This is particularly the case with respect to the authority of the mother; they *feel too big to be governed by a woman*; and if obliged to obey, they will be sullen about it. Instead of requiting her care, by studying to be helpful – anticipating her wishes – they seem to lose all sense of obligation, and regard what she requires of them as an unreasonable interference with their pleasures; and so, they will meet her requests in a snarling, snappish manner, like an impertinent young mastiff, slighting, in every possible way, the thing to be done. And if, in the Providence of God, such boys are left without a father, they take advantage of the widowhood of their mother, to resist her authority. I can scarcely think of anything more *unmanly* than this. It is *mean* and *despicable*. The mother, by all the ties of gratitude, in these desolate circumstances, is entitled to the kindness, assistance, and protection, of her sons; and to rebel against her authority, because she may not have strength to enforce it, manifests a very *black heart*. A young man, who, in any circumstances, will treat his mother ill, is to be despised; but one who will take advantage of the helplessness of her widowhood, to cast off her just authority, is to be detested and abhorred.

Nothing has, perhaps, a greater influence upon the future character of the *man* than the trait of which we are speaking. The boy that is obedient and submissive to parental authority will make a good citizen. He has learned to *obey*, from his childhood; and he

will be obedient to the laws of his country; he will be respected in
society, and may rise to posts of honor. But the disobedient boy,
who is turbulent and ungovernable at home, will make a bad member of society. Never having learned how to obey, he will be disobedient to the laws, and incur their penalty; he will be found in
evil company; engaged in mobs and riots; making disturbance at
fires, etc., till, perhaps, he will land at last in prison, or be launched
into eternity from the gallows. I might easily fill the rest of this
volume with the detail of cases, in which a career of crime, ending in prison or on the gallows, has been commenced in disobedience to parents, and in very many cases, disobedience to widowed
mothers.

⚘ A black spot

Filial piety adds a peculiar charm to the female character; while
the want of it, in females, makes them appear like monsters. Disobedience, or the want of proper respect and reverence to parents,
is so contrary to the gentle nature of your sex, that it makes them
appear very unlovely. This defect needs but to be seen, in a girl
or a young lady, to spoil all her attractions. No matter how beautiful she is – this defect will be a *black spot* on her pretty face; no
matter how much she *knows* – her knowledge, if it does not lead
1 Cor. 8:1 her to honor her parents, only "puffeth up"; no matter how genteel she may be in her behavior to others – the first step in gentility
is, respectful and obedient carriage toward parents. True gentility
comes from gentleness of heart; but there can be no gentleness
in that female heart which dishonors her parents. No matter with
how much elegance and taste she may decorate her beautiful form
– this defect will make her appear worse than the most deformed

person, clad in tattered garments made up of dirty old shreds and patches. Nor will it be confined to childhood and youth; there is, perhaps, nothing that has a more important bearing upon the future character of children and youth than their treatment of their parents. God has set a mark upon it – a good one, upon filial piety, but the mark of Cain upon filial impiety. This latter will stick to you, like a deep, broad scar upon your pretty face, or a permanent deformity in your naturally fine form. But a quick perception of propriety, in regard to the respect due to parents; with a constant watchfulness to show attention, and to anticipate their wants, will adorn a young lady, in the view of all beholders, more than all the finery, and jewels, and other ornaments, that can be heaped upon her. It will make her appear more beautiful than the finest form that was ever beheld, or the most comely countenance that was ever reflected in a mirror.

CHAPTER 5

❧ TREATMENT OF BROTHERS & SISTERS, AND OTHERS IN THE FAMILY

Character formed in the family

The family is a little kingdom in miniature. The father and mother are king and queen; and children, and others residing in the family, are the subjects. I have treated at large, in the last chapter, on your duties to your parents; but I must not pass over your behavior towards the other members of the family. And here, I wish you to keep in mind all I have said about the *formation of character*. Remember, that the character you form in the family will, in all probability, follow you through life. As you are regarded by your own brothers and sisters at home, so, in a great measure, will you be regarded by others, when you leave your father's house. If you are manly, amiable, kind, and courteous, at home, so you will continue to be; and these traits of character will always make you beloved. But if you are peevish, ill-natured, harsh, uncourteous, or overbearing, at home, among your own brothers and sisters, so will you be abroad; and, instead of being beloved, you will be disliked and shunned.

The golden rule

The best general direction that I can give is, that you carry out the golden rule in your behavior toward your brothers and sisters, and all other persons who reside in the family. If you do to them as you would wish them to do to you, all will be well. But I must be a little more particular. Boys are often disposed to assume a dictatorial, domineering air toward their sisters, as though they thought themselves born to rule, and were determined to exercise their dominion over their sisters, because they have not strength to resist their tyranny. But I can hardly think of anything more unmanly. It shows a very mean spirit, destitute of noble and generous feelings, to take advantage of the weakness of others to tyrannize over them. But to do this to those who, by the relation they bear to you, are entitled to your love and protection, is base beyond description. The same is true, though perhaps in a less degree, in regard to the conduct of an elder toward a younger brother.

Behavior to sisters

A brother should be kind, tender, courteous, and delicate, in his behavior toward his sisters, never treating them with rudeness or neglect, and standing ready always to protect them from the rudeness of other boys. He should never speak gruffly to them, nor in a lordly, domineering, or contemptuous manner. Such conduct toward other misses or young ladies would be esteemed very unhandsome and ungentlemanly; and why should it not be so esteemed at home? Are your own sisters entitled to less respect than strangers?

Accustom yourself to make confidants of your sisters. Let them understand your feelings, and know your designs; and pay a suitable regard to their advice. By this means you may be saved from many a snare, and you will secure their affection and sympathy. Never form any design, or engage in any enterprise, which you are ashamed to divulge to them. If you do, you may be sure it will not end well.

Complaining of each other

One rule, well observed at home, among brothers and sisters, would go far towards making them accomplished gentlemen and ladies, in their manners: BE COURTEOUS TO EACH OTHER. Never allow yourself to treat your brothers or sisters in a manner that would be considered rude or ungentlemanly, if done to other young persons visiting in the family. Especially, never allow yourself to play tricks upon them, to tease them, or, in a coarse, rough manner, to criticize or ridicule their conduct, especially in the presence of others. But if you see anything that you think needs reforming, kindly remind them of it in private. This will have a much better effect than if you mortify them, by exposing their faults before company. Be careful of their feelings, and never needlessly injure them.

Boys sometimes take delight in crossing the feelings of their brothers and sisters, interfering with their plans, and vexing them, out of sheer mischief. Such conduct is especially unamiable, and it will tend to promote ill will and contention in the family. Be not fond of informing against them. If they do anything very much amiss, it will be your duty to acquaint your parents with it. But in little things, of small moment, it is better for you kindly to remonstrate with them, but not to appeal to your parents. In some families, when the children are at home, your ears are continually ringing with the unwelcome sounds, "Mother, John" – "Father, Susan" – "Mother, George," etc. – a perpetual string of complaints, which makes the place more like a bedlam than a quiet, sweet home. There is no sight more unlovely than a quarrelsome family – no place on earth more undesirable than a family of brothers and sisters who are perpetually contending with each other. But I know of no place, this side heaven, so sweet and attractive as the home of a family of brothers and sisters, always smiling and happy, full of kindness and love, delighting in each other's happiness, and striving how much each can oblige the other. If you would have your home such a place, you must not be selfish; you must not be too particular about maintaining your own rights; but be ready always to yield rather than to contend. This will generally have the effect to produce the same disposition in your brothers and sisters; and then the strife will be, which can be most generous.

Treatment of domestics

Be noble and generous in your treatment of domestics. Never be so mean as to domineer over the hired men or women employed about the house, or in the field. Keep out of the kitchen as much as possible. But if you are obliged to go there, remember that you are on the cook's premises. Keep out of her way, and be careful not to put things out of their place, or make litter. Nothing is more annoying to her than such conduct, because it interferes with her efforts to keep things in order, and increases her labor. Never ask servants to help you, when you are able to help yourself. It is very provoking to them to be called to wait on the little *gentlemen* about house. Cultivate independence of character, and help yourself. You will never be fit for any business, if you always depend on others to help you in little everyday affairs.

Love of home

Young men and boys should cultivate a *love of home* as a defence against the temptations to frequent bad company and places of resort dangerous to their morals. A boy or a young man, who is deeply and warmly attached to his mother and sisters, will prefer their society to that of the depraved and worthless; and he will not be tempted to go abroad in search of pleasure, when he finds so much at home. It is a delusive idea, that any greater pleasure can be found abroad than is to be enjoyed at home; and that boy or young man is in a dangerous way, to whom the society of his mother and sisters has become insipid and uninteresting. When you feel any inclination to go abroad in search of forbidden pleasure, I advise you to sit down with your sisters, and sing, *"Home, sweet home."* And here I may say that the cultivation of music will add much to the attractions of home. It is a delightful recreation. It soothes the feelings, sweetens the temper, and refines the taste. In addition to the cultivation of the voice, and the practice of vocal music, you will find great satisfaction in learning to play on some instrument of music, to be able to carry your part on the flute or viol. This will greatly diminish the temptation to go abroad for amusement; and in proportion as you find your pleasure at home, will you be safe from those evil influences which have proved the destruction of so many boys.

The only son

But perhaps you are an *only child*. Then you will enjoy the exclusive affections and attention of your parents, without a rival. But you will lose the advantage of the society of brothers and sisters. The former will be no benefit; for parents do not abate their love to their firstborn, when others are added to their number. But the exclusive love to an only child often degenerates into excessive indulgence. The society of brothers and sisters, though it often tries the temper, yet contributes greatly to the happiness of a child. It provides a wholesome discipline, and affords the means of learning how to behave among equals; which an only child cannot learn at home. You will be likely to think too much of yourself, because you will receive the exclusive attentions of your parents, and will not have before you the daily example of your equals. These things you must guard against; and endeavor to make up the deficiency, by carrying out the hints I have given, in the society of other children, wherever you meet them.

In conclusion, I will give you one little *family rule*. You may think it a *very little* one; but it is able to do wonders. If you will try it one week, and never deviate from it, I will promise you the happiest week you ever enjoyed. And, more than this, you will diffuse such a sunshine about you as to make others happy also. My little rule is this: NEVER BE CROSS.

CHAPTER 5

℘ TREATMENT OF BROTHERS & SISTERS, AND OTHERS IN THE FAMILY

Importance of daughters

The happiness of a family depends very much on the conduct of the daughters. They can make home sweet and pleasant. If they are sweet-tempered and amiable, kind and obliging, they will always make it sunshine about them. But, if they are peevish and fretful, selfish and quarrelsome, they will make home as cold and cheerless as a northeast storm. To make home a pleasant, sunshiny place, the family must be governed by the golden rule. If the daughters govern themselves by it, they will be able to shed about the fireside an air of cheerfulness and benignity, that will charm everyone who comes within the circle of its influence.

Eldest sister

If you are the eldest sister, your situation in the family is one of considerable importance and responsibility. Your conduct and example will have a great influence upon your younger brothers and sisters. But you must guard against making too much of this distinction, and expecting too much deference to be paid to you on account of it. You will be tempted to be overbearing and tyrannical in your demeanor toward them. You must guard against this. Your situation in the family, though it entitles you to some deference and respect, yet does not give you any authority; and therefore you must maintain it by the arts of persuasion and kindness. All attempts to domineer over your younger brothers and sisters, will only lead them to treat your pretensions with contempt. But if you speak kindly to them, and show yourself ready to oblige them, and help them out of their little difficulties, you will acquire an influence over them that will be better than authority. It is said that an elephant may be *led* by a single hair; but I need not tell you how vain must be any attempt to *drive* him. Be always good natured, gentle, and kind. Never speak in a cross tone, nor with an assuming air, and never *command* them. By such means, you will secure their *affections*, which will bind them to you with a silken cord. And, if you never lead them astray, you will also secure their *confidence*, to strengthen this cord. Then you may lead them by it at your pleasure.

If you are a younger sister, you must pay some deference to your brothers and sisters older than yourself. If you have an older brother, always treat him respectfully and confidingly. Endeavor to secure his affections and confidence, so that he will be your guide and protector, whenever you need. Be kind and gentle toward him, always yielding to his wishes, whenever you can do so with propriety; never setting up your own will against his, for the sake of having your own way; and be not particular about your own rights. Never behave pettishly toward him, nor find needless fault with him. A sister's power over her brothers lies in her gentleness and sweetness of temper. If you always show an amiable, sweet, loving disposition, they will love you, and seek to gratify your wishes.

But, if you attempt to carry your point by contention, they will shun you, as one who only interferes with their enjoyment.

Make a friend and confidant of your eldest sister. Consult her wishes, and yield to her, when any difference arises between you.

Angels of peace

And, in general, sisters should be angels of mercy and peace in a family – gentle, kind, affectionate, tender, and good-natured, toward all. Make it an invariable rule never to contend; and if you see the beginning of strife, always be the peacemaker – act the part of a mediator, by offering your services to bring about a good understanding between those that are at variance. Never raise your voice so high as to give it the appearance of harshness. Suppress the first
Eccl. 7:9 risings of angry feeling, remembering that "anger resteth in the bosom of fools." Never speak unkindly to your brothers or sisters; and if they speak unkindly to you, do not suffer yourself to be irritated, and to answer back in an angry tone, but show your superiority by controlling your feelings. Be helpful to all about you. If your little brother comes in cold, or wet, or tired, assist him to a seat, take off his outer garments, warm his hands, and make him comfortable. If your little sister is grieved, or in trouble, do not speak harshly to her, or reproach her for crying, but try to soothe her feelings, by diverting her attention. Never tease your brothers or sisters. You do not like to be teased; then do not tease others. Be courteous. Do not speak coarsely or roughly, as ill-bred children do to each other; but be a lady, and treat your brothers and sisters like little gentlemen and ladies. Employ no coarse jokes or vulgar jests. Be careful of their feelings. Never do anything, needlessly, to interfere with their plans, to cross their feelings, or to hold them up to the

ridicule of others; and play no tricks upon them. Such things will diminish their affection, and they will seize the first opportunity to retaliate. Be not fond of informing against them. If they commit any great offence against your parents' authority, it will be your duty to inform them of it. But then you should do it in a very careful manner, not exaggerating, or making it worse than it is, nor speaking of it exultingly or harshly; but show, by your manner, that you are really sorry for the necessity you are under of performing a painful duty. But, in matters of little consequence, it is better for you to remonstrate kindly and tenderly with them, but not to appeal to your parents. If you do, it will occur so frequently that you will get the settled ill will of your brothers and sisters. In some families, you can hear little else, when all the children are at home, but "Mother, James" – "Mother, Mary" – "Mother, Thomas" – "Mother, Sarah" – a perpetual string of complaints, that makes the place more like a bedlam than a quiet, sweet home. If your little brother comes along in a pettish mood, and gives you a gentle slap, half in earnest and half in fun, do not cry out, *"Mother, John's pounding me!"* but take no notice of it, and presently, when he gets better natured, he will be sorry, and perhaps come of his own accord and ask your pardon; or at least, show, by infallible signs, that he wants to *make friends* with you. But if you bristle up, and make a great ado about it, you will have trouble enough. There is no sight more unlovely than a quarrelsome family – no place on earth more undesirable than a family of brothers and sisters, who are perpetually contending with one another. But there is no place, this side heaven, so sweet and attractive, as a family of brothers and sisters always smiling and happy, full of kindness and love, delighting in each other's happiness, and striving how much each can oblige the other.

The only daughter

But perhaps you are an *only child*. Then you will not have some of the trials common to youth. You will not have to strive against those clashing interests and feelings which exist in a large family of brothers and sisters. Your temper will not be put to such trials. But these trials are necessary, in order to discipline the heart, and to teach you the duties growing out of the different relations in life; and you will have them first to encounter abroad, when you come in contact with other girls. You will be greatly in danger of becoming selfish and consequential. Having no rivals in your parents' affections and attentions, you will naturally feel as if you were a person of some consequence, and will, very likely, set a higher value upon yourself than your companions will be willing to acknowledge. Nothing is more liable to give young persons false notions of their own superiority, than being brought up alone, with no opportunity to contrast themselves, daily, with others near their own age.

Treatment of domestics

Be generous in your treatment of domestics. Nothing appears more unlovely than to see a pert little miss domineering over a woman who is employed in doing the work of the house. It is mean and despicable. Such persons have many unpleasant duties to perform; and it should be your aim to render their situation as agreeable and pleasant as possible. Never presume to *command* them. This does not belong to you. If you need their help, request it as a favor; but never ask them to do anything for you, which you can do yourself. If you have everything done for you, it will make you helpless. It is much better for you to learn to help yourself; and women that do work in a family do not like to wait on children who are able to wait on themselves. Indeed, you ought to make it a rule, never to ask anyone to do that for you which you can do yourself. If you make yourself dependent upon others, you will be troublesome wherever you go, and an unwelcome guest among your friends. But do not be very familiar with hired men or women, nor make them your companions or confidants; for they may lead you astray.

~

In conclusion, I will give you one little *family rule*. You may think it a *very little* one; but it is able to do wonders. If you will try it one week, and never deviate from it, I will promise you the happiest week you ever enjoyed. And, more than this, you will diffuse such a sunshine about you as to make others happy also. My little rule is this: NEVER BE CROSS.

CHAPTER 6

BEHAVIOR AT SCHOOL

Honoring teachers

Most of what I have said in the last two chapters will apply to your behavior at school. When you go to school, your teachers take the place of your parents. To them, for the time being, your parents have delegated their authority. You are bound, therefore, to give to them the same reverence and obedience which are due to your parents. To disobey, or to dishonor them in any other way, is a breach of the fifth commandment, which, in its spirit, requires *subordination to lawful authority*; or, as the Catechism says, "The fifth commandment requireth the preserving the honor of, and performing the duties belonging to, everyone, in their several places and relations, as superiors, inferiors, or equals." You ought, therefore, in the first place, to pay strict regard to every rule of the school, as a religious duty; and obey your teacher, in all things, with the same promptness and cheerfulness that you would obey your parents. You should be too careful of your own reputation to permit yourself to be reprimanded by your teacher. If you take up the resolution that you will be so diligent, faithful, and well-behaved, as never to be reproved, you will find it a very wholesome restraint, to keep you within the bounds of propriety. Be careful

Westminster
Shorter
Catechism,
A 64

38

of the *honor* of your teachers, remembering that, if you dishonor them, you break God's holy commandment. Never call in question their arrangements; and never indulge feelings of dissatisfaction. Especially, never speak slightingly or disrespectfully of them, nor of their ways. It does not become you to call in question their arrangements, or their mode of teaching. If you are wiser than they, you had better not seek instruction from them; but if not, then you should be satisfied with the dictates of their superior wisdom. Never attempt to question their proceedings, nor to argue with them, when they require you to do anything. Be very careful, also, not to carry home tales from school; because such a practice tends to cultivate a disposition to tattle, and often leads to great mischief. Yet, when your parents make inquiries, it is your duty to answer them.

Diligence in study

Be diligent in your studies, from *principle*, not from a spirit of emulation. Remember that you are placed at school for your own benefit. It is not for your parents' advantage, nor for the benefit of your teachers, that you are required to study; but for your own good. Remember how much pains your parents take, to give you this opportunity. They give up your time, which they have a right to employ for their own benefit, and they expend money for the support of schools, that you may have the opportunity of obtaining useful learning. You are bound, therefore, to improve this opportunity with great diligence. You will not think it a task, that you are compelled to study; but you will regard it as a price put into your hands to get wisdom. It is all for your own benefit. In school hours, therefore, you should put away all thoughts of play, and all communication with other scholars, and give yourself strictly and closely to your studies. Prov. 17:16

℘ Lingering by the way

But, I suppose you will find the most difficulty in regulating your conduct during the intervals of school hours, and on your way to and from school. When a great many young persons of your own age are together, there is a disposition to throw off restraint. I would not have you under such restraint as to avoid all relaxation and innocent hilarity; for these are necessary to keep your mind and body in a healthful condition. But, here, you will be more exposed to temptation. As punctuality is of great importance in school, and a necessary habit to be cultivated, you need to make it a matter of principle to be always in your seat a few minutes before the opening of school. A failure to do this, will rob you of many advantages, and greatly embarrass your teacher. It will, also, give you the habit of tardiness, which will be a great injury to you, as long as you live, whatever may be your occupation. But, in order to be punctual, you must not linger to engage in sport by the way. So, likewise, in returning from school, you ought to be equally punctual in reporting yourself at home; for you know not what your parents may have for you to do. This, also, forbids your lingering for amusement on the way home. But, besides these, there are other reasons why you should not idle away your time on the way. Idle boys are always in the way of temptation; for

Isaac Watts,
Divine &
Moral Songs,
"Against
Idleness
& Mischief"

> "Satan finds some mischief still
> For idle hands to do."

If you linger along on the way, you will be very likely to meet with some bad boys, who will lead you astray, and involve you in some mischief that will get you into serious difficulty. A boy was walking along in the streets of Boston, and another boy, who knew

him by name, called to him from the other side of the street, saying, "Come, John, come over here, and we'll have some fun." "No,
I can't," John replied; "I must go home." "But just come over here
a minute." "No, I can't," said John; "my mother expects me home."
But the boy still urged him, and at length prevailed on him to cross
the street. They then went into a hardware store; and the boy who
called John over stole some knives and disappeared; and John was
taken for the theft, because he was with the other boy at the time,
and put in jail. Thus, by just stopping on the way, and going across
the street, he got into jail. If he had made it his invariable rule to
go directly on his way, and not linger, and idle his time away, he
would have been saved from this suffering, shame, and disgrace.
But, if you indulge in the same habit of lingering by the way, you
will be exposed to similar temptation and trouble.

ࣴ Being gentlemanly

In all your intercourse with your schoolfellows, be kind and obliging. Treat them courteously, and avoid everything that is rough,
coarse, and rude. Endeavor to behave like a *young gentleman*. Avoid
the company of boys who are rough and coarse in their manners,
or profane or obscene in their conversation. You will insensibly
imbibe their vulgarity, if you associate with them. In your sports
or plays, be conscientiously fair and honorable. The boy, who is
unfair or dishonest in his play, when he becomes a man, will drive
a hard bargain or be dishonest in his business.

If you go where boys and girls are associated in the same school,
have a strict regard to propriety, in your intercourse with the other
sex. Be gentlemanly in your behavior towards them. Avoid all rudeness or roughness of manners and conversation in their presence.
Especially, refrain from rude jests and low buffoonery. You may

engage with them in sensible conversation; but a well-bred girl
will be offended if you attempt to please her by trying how non-
sensically and silly you can talk. Venture no improper liberties; but
maintain your own self-respect by respecting them.

Finally, see that you do nothing in school or out of it, which
you would be unwilling your parents should see; and remember
that there is One Eye that is always upon you.

General behavior

But, I suppose you will find the most difficulty in regulating your
conduct during the intervals of school hours, and on your way
to and from school. When a great many young persons of your
own age are together, there is a disposition to throw off restraint. I
would not have you under such restraint as to avoid all relaxation
and innocent hilarity; for these are necessary to keep your mind
and body in a healthful condition. But you must be careful to do
nothing inconsistent with propriety – nothing out of character for
your sex. If you go to a school composed of both sexes, as most
of our country schools are, it would be unbecoming in you to play
with the boys, or to associate with them, any further than to engage
in modest and sensible conversation, which will be improving and
profitable both to them and to yourself. But the sports in which
boys usually engage are improper for your sex; and for you to engage in rude, boisterous conversation and coarse jesting, such as
ill-bred youth are wont to practice, would be highly unbecoming.
You ought to carry out the rules of good breeding, in all your intercourse with your fellow pupils. Be kind, courteous, affable, and
obliging toward all. Treat them as your brothers and sisters, except
to maintain more reserve than you do at home, especially towards

those of the other sex. You must not allow boys to be too familiar; but be modest, and keep them at a respectful distance. And if they are inclined to be rude and unmannerly, have nothing at all to say to them. Choose for your recreations, those sports which are gentle and suited to your sex, not rough and roisterous. Be especially careful of your conduct on the way, to and from school. Make it a principle always to be at school in time; and never linger by the way, either going or coming, for this will destroy your habits of punctuality, and expose you to many bad influences. It is of the utmost consequence to be punctual at school hours. All the affairs of the school are deranged by tardiness; and you not only suffer loss in your recitations, but in your habits.

A wormhole in a ship

There is often much impropriety practised at the intervals of school hours, and on the way to and from school; and there is great danger that thoughtless girls will lose their delicacy, and have their principles undermined, before they are aware of it. A man was at work in a shipyard, in company with other men, in the building of a vessel. He was preparing one of the planks for the bottom of the ship. "There," said he to his comrades, "is a wormhole," as he planed off the rough outside of the plank. The workmen examined it, but concluded the hole was so small it could never do any injury. The plank was put in the vessel. Some years afterwards, as that ship was at sea, there came up a violent storm, and the ship sprung a leak. On examining the bottom, it was found that the water had for a long time soaked into a wormhole, and rotted the wood for some distance around, till now, in the time of trial, when the waves beat furiously against the ship, it had suddenly given way. The men on board made every exertion to get her ashore, but were obliged to abandon her, and she sunk to rise no more. Many a girl has been ruined in consequence of a very slight deviation from propriety, which has led on to others of a more serious nature, till, at length, her principles have been corrupted, and in the hour of temptation they have given way, and she has sunk to rise no more! A sad warning to others to watch against the *beginnings of evil*. It is the "little foxes," as Solomon says, that "spoil the vines." The old foxes eat the grapes; but the little foxes, running on the tender parts of the vines, as they put forth to bud and blossom, spoil them before the fruit grows. It is thus that the character is corrupted and secretly undermined, by little causes, in early life. When a girl consents, in a single instance, to step beyond the bounds of propriety, she exposes herself to the most imminent danger of ruin. The following rule, if adhered to, will save you from a multitude of evils, while out of your parents' sight: ALWAYS CONDUCT AS YOU WOULD IF YOU WERE UNDER THE EYE OF YOUR PARENTS, AND NEVER FORGET THE ONE EYE THAT IS ALWAYS UPON YOU.

Cant. 2:15

CHAPTER 7

BEHAVIOR AT TABLE

Importance of mealtime

Did it ever occur to you to inquire why all civilized people have their food prepared at particular hours, and all the family sit at table together? Why not have the food prepared, and placed where everyone can go and eat, whenever he pleases, by himself? One great advantage of having a whole family sit together, and partake of their meals at the same time, is, that it brings them together in a social way, every day. But for this, and the assembling of the family at prayers, they might not all meet at once for a long time. But eating together is a mark of friendship; and it tends to promote social feeling. In a well-regulated family, also, it is a means of great improvement, both of mind and manners. It is, in fact, a school of good manners. You will perceive, then, how very important it is, that your behavior at table should always be regulated by the rules of propriety. If you acquire vulgar habits here, or practise rudeness, you will find it difficult to overcome them; and they will make you appear to great disadvantage.

I shall mention a few things to be observed, at the table, by one who would maintain a character for good breeding. And, first of all, be not tardy in taking your place at the table. In a well-regulated family, the master of the family waits till all are seated before he asks a blessing. Suppose there are five persons at the table, and you hinder them all by your tardiness three minutes, you waste fifteen minutes of precious time. To those who set a proper value upon time, this is a great evil. There is no need of it; you may as easily be at your seat in time as too late. When called to a meal, never wait to finish what you are doing, but promptly leave it, and proceed to your place. Above all, do not delay till after the blessing, and so sit down to your food like a heathen.

Table talk

The table is a place for easy, cheerful, social intercourse; but some children make it a place of noisy clamor. The younger members of the family should leave it for the parents (and guests, if there are any) to take the lead in conversation. It does not appear well for a very young person to be forward and talkative at table. You should generally wait till you are spoken to; or, if you wish to make an inquiry or a remark, do it in a modest, unassuming way, not raising your voice, nor spinning out a story. And be especially careful not to interrupt any other person. Sensible people will get a very unfavorable impression concerning you, if they see you bold and talkative at table. Yet you should never appear inattentive to what others are saying. Be not so intent on discussing the contents of your plate, as not to observe the movements of others, or to hear their conversation. Show your interest in what is said by occasional glances at the speaker, and by the expression of your countenance; but be not too anxious to put a word in yourself. Some children make themselves ridiculous, by always joining in, and making their remarks, when older persons are speaking, often giving a grave opinion of some matter about which they know nothing.

Helpfulness

Be helpful to others, without staring at them, or neglecting your own plate. You may keep your eye on the movements around you, to pass a cup and saucer, to notice if anyone near you needs helping, and to help any dish that is within your reach. By so doing, you may greatly relieve your father and mother, who must be very busy, if they help all the family. By cultivating a close observation, and studying to know and anticipate the wants of others, you will be able to do these things in a genteel and graceful manner, without appearing obtrusive or forward.

Propriety

Study *propriety*. If asked what you will be helped to, do not answer in an indefinite manner, saying, you "have no choice"; for this will put the master of the house to the inconvenience of choosing for you. Do not wait, after you are asked, to determine what you will have, but answer promptly; and do not be particular in your choice. To be very particular in the choice of food is not agreeable to good breeding. Never ask for what is not on the table. Do not make re-marks respecting the food; and avoid expressing your likes and dislikes of particular articles. One of your age should not appear to be an epicure. Show your praise of the food set before you, by the good nature and relish with which you partake of it; but do not eat so fast as to appear voracious. Never put on sour looks, nor turn up your nose at your food. This is unmannerly, and a serious affront to the mistress of the table. Be careful to use your knife and fork as other people do, and to know when to lay them down, and when to hold them in your hands. Be careful not to drop your food, nor to spill liquids on the cloth. Do not leave the table before the family withdraw from it, unless it is necessary; and then, ask to be excused. Neither linger to finish your meal, after you perceive the rest have done.

~

Besides what I have mentioned, there are a great many nameless little things, that go to make up good manners at table, which you must learn by studying the rules of propriety, and observing the behavior of others.

CHAPTER 8

BEHAVIOR AT FAMILY WORSHIP

All well-regulated Christian families are assembled, morning and evening, to worship God. Seeing we are dependent on him for all things, it is suitable and proper that we should daily acknowledge our dependence, by asking him for what we need, and thanking him for what we receive. That we should do this *as a family* is highly proper. But if it is our duty to worship God *as a family*, it is the duty of everyone in particular. It is as much your duty as it is your father's. You must, therefore, not only make it a principle to be in your place punctually at the time, but to enter heartily into all the exercises. Some children and youth appear as if they had no interest in what is going on, at this most interesting household service. But this is not only showing great disrespect to your parents, but great irreverence toward God. It will help you to right feelings, on these occasions, if you imagine Christ Jesus present in person. God is present spiritually, and in a peculiar manner, at such times, to bless the families that call on his name. When, therefore, the family are assembled for prayers, you should put away all vain or wandering thoughts. When the time arrives, and the family are assembled for devotion, seat yourself, in a serious, reverent manner; and if there should be a few moments' delay, do not engage in conversation, nor in reading newspapers, or anything calculated to divert your mind; but direct your thoughts upward to God, and seek a preparation for his worship. Suffer not your mind to be occupied with anything but the service before you. Let not your eyes wander about, to catch vagrant thoughts. Let not your hands be occupied with anything, to divert your attention or to disturb others. Have your Bible, and take your turn in reading. Be attentive and devout, during the reading of God's holy word, endeavoring to apply it to your heart. If the family sing, enter into this sweet service, not only with your lips, but with your heart. When prayer is offered, place yourself in the attitude which is taken by your father and mother. If they kneel, do you kneel also – not sit, nor recline, but stand upon your knees, in a reverent posture. Shut your eyes, and keep your heart. Let your heart embrace the words of the prayer, and make them your own. Remember that the devotional habits you form at the family altar, are the habits that will follow you to God's house, and probably adhere to you through life. And what can be more shocking than to see persons pretending to gentility, who do not know how to behave with propriety before the great God that made them! If you were in company, and should treat the person that invited you with as much indifference as you treat God by such conduct, you would be considered a very ill-bred person. He has invited you to come to his mercy seat to converse with him, and to receive favors at his hand; and yet, by such conduct as I have named, you show no interest at all in the matter.

Family devotion, when rightly improved, is a very important means of grace. If you attend upon it seriously and reverently, you may hope that God will bless it to your soul. It tends, also, to tranquillize the feelings, and prepare you to engage in the duties of the day with serenity and cheerfulness.

CHAPTER 9

PRIVATE PRAYER

The prayerless soul

I suppose, if my readers are the children of pious parents, they have been taught from their earliest recollection, to retire, morning and evening, to some secret place, to read their Bible alone, and engage in private prayer. This, in very early childhood, is often an interesting and affecting service. But when young people come to a certain age, if their hearts are not renewed, they are disposed to regard this as an irksome duty, and gradually to leave it off. They find the old adage, in the primer, true – "Praying will make thee leave sinning, and sinning will make thee leave praying."

The New England Primer (c. 1690)

It is a sad period, in the history of a young person, when the early habit of prayer is given up. Then the heart becomes like the garden of the slothful, described by Solomon:

"I went by the field of the slothful, and by the vineyard of the man void of understanding; and lo, it was all grown over with thorns, and nettles had covered the face thereof, and the stone wall thereof was broken down." Prov. 24:30-31

There are no good plants thriving in the prayerless soul; but weeds, and briars, and thorns, grow thick and rank, occupying every vacant spot. The stone wall is broken down: there is no defence against the beasts of the field. Every vagrant thought, every vicious passion, find free admittance. The heart grows hard, and the spirit careless. Sin is not dreaded as it once was. The fear of God and the desire of his favor are gone. "God is not in all his thoughts." That youth stands on the very edge of a frightful precipice.

Psalm 10:4

Excuses

I would not have you think, however, that there is any *merit* in prayer; or that the prayers of one whose "heart is not right with God" are acceptable to him. But, what I say is, that everyone ought to pray to God with a right heart. If your heart is not right with God, then it is wrong; and you are to blame for having it wrong. I will suppose a case, to illustrate what I mean. You see a child rise up in the morning, and go about the house; and though its mother is with it all the time, yet the child neither speaks to her nor seems to notice her at all. After a while, the mother asks what is the matter, and why her dear child does not speak to her? The child says, "I have *no heart* to speak to you, mother. I do not *love* you; and so I think it would be wrong for me to speak to you." What would you think of such conduct? You would say, "The child *ought* to love its mother; and it is only an aggravation of its offence, to carry out the feelings of its heart in its conduct?" "Would you then have it act the hypocrite, and speak with its lips what it does not feel in its heart?" No; but I would have it love its mother, as every dutiful child ought to do, and then act out, in its speech and behavior, what it feels in its heart. But I would never have it excuse itself from right actions because its heart is wrong. Now, apply this to the subject of prayer, and you will see the character of all impenitent excuses for neglecting this duty. And those who go on and continue to neglect it, certainly have no reason to expect that their hearts will grow any better by it, but only worse. But in attempting to perform a sacred duty, the Lord may give you grace to perform it aright, and then you will have a new heart.

How to pray

If possible, have a particular place of prayer, where you can be secure from all interruption, and particular times for it. At the appointed hours, retire alone, and put away all thoughts about your studies, your work, your amusements, or anything of a worldly nature, and try to realize that God is as truly present as if you saw him with your bodily eyes. Then read his word, as though you heard him speaking to you in the sacred page; and when your mind has become serious and collected, kneel down and acknowledge God as your Creator and Preserver, your God and Redeemer; thank him for the mercies you have received, mentioning particularly every good thing you can think of, that you have received from him; confess your sins; plead for pardon, through the blood of Jesus Christ; and ask him to give you such blessings as you see and feel that you need. Pray also for your friends (and for your enemies, if you have any); and conclude with a prayer for the coming of Christ's kingdom every where throughout the world.

Some young people neglect to pray, because they think they are not able to form their words into prayer. But you need not be afraid to speak to God. If you can find language to ask your parents for what you desire, you can find words to express your desires to God; and he will not upbraid you for the imperfection of your language. He looks at the heart. If that is right, your prayer will be accepted.

Let me earnestly entreat you to have your set times for prayer, at least as often as morning and evening; and never suffer yourself to neglect them. And, especially, do not adopt the unseemly practice of saying your prayers in bed, but give to God the brightest and best hours of the day, and not offer to him the blind and the lame for sacrifice. You will find the regular and stated habit of prayer, thus formed in early life, of great value to you, as long as you live.

Benefits of prayer

But let me once more caution you not to trust in your prayers, for they cannot save you; and do not think, because you are regular and habitual in attending to the outward forms of duty, that you must be a Christian.

Prayer, if sincere and true, will prepare you for engaging in the duties of the day, or for enjoying calm repose at night. If, for any cause, you neglect prayer in the morning, you may expect things will go ill with you all the day. You can do nothing well without God's blessing; and you cannot expect his blessing without asking for it. You need, also, that calm, tranquil, humble spirit which prayer promotes, to prepare you to encounter those things which are constantly occurring to try the feelings, and to enable you to do anything well. Therefore, never engage in anything of importance without first seeking direction of God; and never do anything on which you would be unwilling to ask His blessing.

CHAPTER 10

KEEPING THE SABBATH

Benefits of the Sabbath

Some people esteem it a hardship to be compelled to keep the Sabbath. They think it an interference with their liberties, that the state should make laws to punish them for breaking it. This disposition very early shows itself in children. Often they think it is hard that they are restrained from play, or from seeking their pleasure, on the holy Sabbath. But God did not give us the Sabbath for his own sake, or because he is benefited by our keeping it. The Bible says, "The Sabbath was made for man." God gave us the Sabbath for our benefit, and for two purposes. He has made us so that we need rest one day in seven. It has been proved, upon fair trial, that men cannot do as much, nor preserve their health as well, by laboring seven days in a week, as they can by laboring six days, and resting one day in a week. If there were no Sabbath, you would have no day of rest. You would grow weary of school, if you were obliged to attend and study seven days in a week. If you are kept at home to work, you would soon tire out, if you had to labor every day in the week. But, by resting every seventh day, you get recruited, so that you are able to go on with study or work with new vigor. The Sabbath, in this respect, is then a great blessing to you; and you ought

Mark 2:27

to be so thankful to God for it, as to keep it strictly according to his command.

Another object of the Sabbath is, to give all people an opportunity to lay aside their worldly cares and business, to worship God and learn his will. The other design of the Sabbath was, to *benefit the body*; this is, to *bless the soul*. If there were no Sabbath, people that are dependent upon others would be obliged to work every day in the week; and they would have no time to meet together for the worship of God. And, if everyone were allowed to choose his own time for worshipping God, there would be no agreement. One would be at meeting, another would be at work, and others would be seeking their pleasure. But, in order to have everyone at liberty to worship God without disturbance, he has set apart one day in seven for this purpose. On this day, he requires us to rest from all labor and recreation, and spend its sacred hours in learning his will, and in acts of devotion. The Sabbath thus becomes a means of improving the mind and the heart. It furnishes the best opportunity for social improvement that could be devised. It brings the people together, in their best attire, to exercise their minds in understanding divine truth, and their hearts in obeying it. And the same object, and the same spirit, it carries out in the family. If, therefore, you ever consider the duties of the holy Sabbath irksome and unpleasant, or feel uneasy under its restraints, you perceive that you must be very unreasonable, since they are designed for your good. You will not, then, find fault with me, if I am rigid in requiring the strict observance of the Sabbath. One thing I would have you remember: *If you would receive the full benefit of the holy Sabbath, you must form right habits of keeping it, early in life.* To give it full power over the mind, it must be associated, in our earliest recollections, with order, quiet, stillness, and solemnity. If you are in the habit of disregarding it in early life, you lose all the benefit and enjoyment to be derived from these sacred associations.

How to keep the Sabbath

The best directions for keeping the Sabbath, any where to be found, are contained in the thirteenth verse of the fifty-eighth chapter of Isaiah: "If thou turn away thy foot from the Sabbath, from doing thy pleasure on my holy day, and call the Sabbath a delight, the holy of the Lord, honorable; and shalt honor him, not doing thine own ways, nor finding thine own pleasure, nor speaking thine own words—" You must *turn away your foot from the Sabbath*, not trampling on it by doing your own pleasure, instead of the pleasure of the Lord. Your foot must not move to perform any act that is contrary to the design of this sacred day; and especially, must not go after your own pleasure. You must not *do your own ways*, nor *find your own pleasure*. These things may be lawful on other days; but on this day, everything must have reference to God. You must not even *speak your own words*. Worldly, vain, light, or trifling conversation is thus forbidden. And, if you may not speak your own words, you may not think your own thoughts. Worldly, vain, trifling thoughts, or thoughts of your pleasure, are not lawful on God's holy day. But you must not only *refrain* from these things; the Sabbath is not properly kept, unless its sacred services are a *delight* to the soul. If you are tired of hearing, reading, and thinking of the things of another world, you do not keep the Sabbath according to these directions. To one who enters truly into the spirit of God's holy day, it is the most delightful of the seven. You remember, in the memoir of Phebe Bartlett, it is stated that she so loved the Sabbath that she would long to have it come, and count the days intervening before it. Such are the feelings of all who love God and sacred things.

Preparation

Having made these general remarks, I will give you a few simple directions for making the Sabbath both profitable and delightful. The evening before the Sabbath, do everything that can be done, to save doing on the Sabbath. Leave nothing to be done in *God's time* that you can do in your *own time*. Lay out your Sabbath day's clothing, and see that it is all in order, that you may have no brushing or mending to be done Sabbath morning. Rise early in the morning, and, while washing and dressing, which you will do in as little

Titus 3:5 time as possible, think of your need of the "washing of regeneration and renewing of the Holy Ghost," and of being clothed in the clean, white robe of Christ's righteousness. Then offer up your thanksgiving to God for his mercy in preserving your life, and giving you another holy Sabbath, and pray for his presence and blessing through the day. If you are called by your father or mother, for any service of the family, go to it cheerfully; and as soon as you can retire again, read a portion of Scripture, and pray to God for such particular blessings upon yourself as you feel your need of, and for his blessing upon others on his holy day. If you attend the Sabbath school, you will need to look over your lesson for the day, and endeavor to apply it to your own heart; for I suppose you do not put off the study of your lesson till Sabbath morning.

Going to meeting

Never stay at home on the Sabbath, unless you are necessarily detained. Make it a matter of principle and calculation always to be there. On your way to the house of God, do not engage in any un-

necessary conversation, especially that which is vain, light, or trifling, to divert your mind, and unfit you for the worship of God.
Do not stand about the doors of the meetinghouse, to salute your
friends, or to converse with your young companions. This practice,
I am sorry to say, prevails in the country, among young people of
both sexes, to the great annoyance of well-bred people. It is a great
temptation to conversation improper for the Sabbath. It is very unpleasant for people who are passing, to have the way blocked up,
so as to have to press through a crowd. Neither do people like to
be *stared at*, by a company of rude young people, as they pass into
the house of God. I am sorry to admit, also, that this unmannerly
practice is not confined to youth; but that many elderly people set
the example. Instead of doing so, go directly to your seat, in a quiet,
reverent manner; and if any time intervenes before the commence-
ment of public worship, do not spend it in gazing about the house,
to observe the dress of different persons; but take the opportunity
to compose your mind, to call in all vagrant thoughts, to get your
heart impressed with a sense of God's presence, and to lift up your
soul in silent prayer for his blessing. Or, if the time be long, you
can employ a part of it in reading the Bible, or devotional hymns.
But do not carry any other book to the house of worship to be read
there. If you have a Sabbath school library book, it will be better
not to read it at such a time, because you will be likely to get your
mind filled with it, so as to interfere with the services of the sanctu-
ary. But the Bible and hymn book, being of a devotional character,
will tend to prepare your mind for worship. Above all, do not read
a newspaper, of any kind, at such a time. Even a religious newspaper would tend to divert your mind from that serious, tender,
devout frame, which you ought to possess when you engage in the
solemn public worship of the Great Jehovah. But I have often wit-

nessed more serious improprieties, in the house of God, than any of these. I have seen young people whispering and laughing during the sermon; and it is a very common thing to see them gazing about during the singing, as though they had nothing to do with the service. I have also seen them engaged in reading, in the time of sermon, or of singing. Some, also, are seen, in time of prayer, with their eyes wide open, gazing about. Such conduct would be very unmannerly, if nobody were concerned but the minister; for it is treating him as though he were not worthy of your attention. But when it is considered that he speaks to you *in the name of God*, and that, in prayer, while you stand up with the congregation, you profess to join in the prayer; and while the hymn is sung, you profess to exercise the devout feeling which it expresses – when all these things are considered, such conduct as that I have described appears impious in a high degree.

Instead of being guilty of such improprieties, you will endeavor, from the heart, to join in the sentiments expressed in prayer and praise; and listen to the sermon with all attention, as a message sent from God to you. You must not think that the sermon is designed for older people, and therefore you have nothing to do with it; nor take up the notion that sermons are too dry and uninteresting to engage your attention. The minister speaks *to you*, in the name of God, those great truths which concern the salvation of the soul. Can they be of no interest to you? Have you not a soul to be saved or lost? Nor need you think that you cannot understand the sermon. If you *give your attention*, you can understand a sermon as well as you can understand the lessons you are required every day to study at school. If you do not understand preaching, it is because you do not give your mind to it, and hear with attention. Your mind is here and there, "walking to and fro in the earth, _{Job 1:7, 2:2} and going up and down in it"; and you only catch, here and there, a sentence of the sermon. This is the reason you do not understand it. Endeavor to examine your heart and life by what you hear, and to apply it to yourself in such a way as to be benefitted by it. And, when you leave the house of God, do not immediately engage in conversation, and by this means dissipate all impression; but, as far as possible, go home in silence, and retire to your closet, to seek the blessing of God upon the services of his house, on which you have attended.

Sabbath school

I suppose, of course, that you attend the Sabbath school. I think it a great advantage to those who rightly improve it. But, like every other privilege, it may be so neglected or abused as to be of no benefit. If you pay no attention to the Sabbath school lesson at home, your mere attendance upon the recitation at school will do you little good. You will feel little interest, and receive little profit. But, if you make it the occasion for the faithful study of the Holy Scriptures at home, to ascertain their meaning, and to become acquainted with the great truths of Christianity, it will be of great service to you in forming your Christian character.

Having well and thoroughly studied your Sabbath school lesson, you will then be prepared to engage in the recitation with interest. In the Sabbath school, you will observe the same general directions for propriety of behavior as in public worship. You are to remember that it is the holy Sabbath, and that the Sabbath school is a religious meeting. All lightness of manner is out of place. A serious deportment is necessary, if you would profit by it. Courtesy to your teacher, and to the school, also requires that you should give your attention, and not be conversing or reading during the recitation, or while your teacher is speaking to you. In answering the questions, you should be full and explicit; not merely making the briefest possible reply, but entering into the subject with interest. But be careful that you do not give indulgence to a self-confident, conceited spirit, nor appear as if you thought yourself wiser than your teacher. Such a spirit indulged will have an injurious influence in the formation of your character, and will make you an object of disgust to sensible people.

Some young people, when a little past the period of childhood, begin to feel as if they were too old to attend the Sabbath school, and so gradually absent themselves, and finally leave it altogether. This arises from a mistaken notion as to the design of the Sabbath school. It is not a school *for children merely*; but a school for all classes of people, to engage in the study of the most wonderful book in the world. I hope you will never think of leaving the Sabbath school, as long as you are able to attend it. If you do, you will suffer a loss which you will regret as long as you live.

Sabbath noon

If you remain at the house of worship between the Sabbath school and the afternoon service, as many do in the country, you will be exposed to temptations to profane the Sabbath. To prevent this, avoid meeting with your companions, in groups, for conversation. However well disposed you may be, you can hardly avoid being drawn into conversation unsuitable for the holy Sabbath. If you take a book from the Sabbath school library, this will be a suitable time to read it, if you are careful not to extend the reading into the afternoon service, or suffer your thoughts to be diverted by what you have read. But the practice of reading the Sabbath school books during divine service, which prevails among children, and even with some young men and women, is not only very irreverent, but a gross violation of good breeding. It is slighting the service of God, and treating the minister as though they thought what he has to say to them not worth their attention.

Sabbath afternoon and evening

You ought to have a particular time set apart for the study of your Sabbath school lesson. I should prefer that this be taken during the week, so as not to task your mind too severely on the Sabbath with *study*, inasmuch as it is a day of *rest*. But, if you cannot do this, I should advise that you study it Sabbath afternoon, and review it the next Sabbath morning.

Some portion of the Sabbath afternoon, or evening, you will employ, under the direction of your parents, in repeating the Catechism, which, I hope none of my readers will consider beneath their attention. *The Shorter Catechism*, next to the Bible, I regard as the best book in existence to lay the foundation of a strong and solid religious character. If you get it thoroughly committed to memory, so as to be able to repeat it verbatim from beginning to end, you will never regret it; but, as long as you live, you will have occasion to rejoice in it. I cannot now give you any adequate idea of the benefit you will derive from it. These catechetical exercises in your father's house will be associated, in your mind, with the most precious recollections of your early years. As I said with regard to your Sabbath school lessons, and for the same reason, I should advise you, if possible, to study the portion of the Catechism to be recited, during the week. But if you cannot do so, it should be studied on the afternoon or evening of the Sabbath. If, however, you study these lessons in the week time, you will be able to spend the afternoon and evening of the Sabbath, except what is devoted to family worship and repeating the Catechism, in reading serious and devotional books, which will not tax your mind so much. If you are engaged in study all the week, your mind will need rest. Therefore, I would have you prosecute your *religious study* during the week, and let your mind be taxed less on the Sabbath, reading such books and engaging in such services as are calculated more to affect the heart, than to tax the mind. You ought to spend more time than usual, on God's holy day, in your closet, in reading the Scriptures and prayer. But, besides the Bible, I would particularly recommend Religious Biographies, and such works as Bunyan's *Pilgrim's Progress* and *Holy War*, D'Aubigne's *History of the Reformation*, etc. But secular history, or any books or papers of a secular character, should not be read on the holy Sabbath. In general, you may safely read, on Sabbath afternoon, the books that you find in the Sabbath school library; though it will sometimes happen that a book creeps into the library that is not suitable for this sacred day. A portion of the evening of the Sabbath, before retiring to rest, should be spent in reviewing the day, recollecting the sermons, examining how you have kept the day, and seeking in prayer the pardon of what has been amiss, and God's blessing on all the services in which you have been engaged.

Those blest who keep the Sabbath

A Sabbath thus spent will be a blessing to you, not only for the six days following, but as long as you live. It will contribute to the formation of religious habits that you will be thankful for to the day of your death. And when you become accustomed to spending your

Sabbaths thus, so far from finding them long and tedious days, you will find them the most delightful of the seven, and will only regret that they are TOO SHORT – they come to an end before you have finished all the good designs you have formed.

The fact that God has set apart a day to himself, and commanded us to keep it holy, would naturally lead us to conclude that he would order his Providence so as to favor its observance. We have only need to examine the subject to be convinced that he does so. When his ancient people, the children of Israel, refused to keep his Sabbaths, and trampled his holy day under foot, he emptied them out of the land, and caused them to be carried off into a strange country, and to remain there seventy years. This was threatened in Leviticus 26:34–35: "Then shall the land enjoy her Sabbaths, as long as it lieth desolate, and ye be in your enemies' land; even then shall the land rest, and enjoy her Sabbaths. As long as it lieth desolate, it shall rest; because it did not rest in your Sabbaths, when ye dwelt upon it." In 2 Chronicles 36:20–21, this is referred to as one of the principal reasons why they were carried away to Babylon: "And them that escaped the sword carried he away to Babylon; where they were servants to him and his sons, until the reign of the kingdom of Persia, to fulfil the word of the Lord by the mouth of Jeremiah the prophet, until the land had enjoyed her Sabbaths; for as long as she lay desolate, she kept Sabbath, to fulfil threescore and ten years."

I can think of no reason why God, in his holy Providence, should not punish Sabbath-breakers now as well as then. I have no doubt that he does. If we could see the design of his Providence, as it is explained in the Bible, no one would doubt it. Sir Matthew Hale, after a long and laborious public life, declared, as the result of his experience, that he found his affairs prosper, during the week, just in proportion to the strictness with which he had observed the Sabbath; and that he had never met with success in any business which was planned on the Sabbath.

I might fill this book with narratives of accidents that have happened to young people, while seeking their pleasure on the Lord's day. Scarcely a week occurs, in the summer season, but the papers contain accounts of parties of young people drowned while taking Sabbath excursions on the water, or of young men and boys drowned while bathing on the Lord's day. Many very striking accounts of this kind have been collected and published in tracts. And a great many facts of a more general nature have also been published, in various forms, showing that it is *profitable* to keep the Sabbath, and *unprofitable* and dangerous to break it. My object, in this place, is simply to impress on the minds of my readers the very important influence which the proper observance of the Sabbath has in the *formation of character*. And I wish them to follow the youth through life who has been accustomed to keep the Sabbath, and who continues to keep it; and then follow the course of one who has, in early life, been accustomed to disregard God's holy day. And one thought, in particular, I desire you to ponder well – *The Sabbath-breaker cannot expect God's protection*. And, if God forsakes you, what will become of you?

A party of young people set out for a sail, on the Sabbath day. One of the young ladies told her brother that she felt very bad to think she was breaking the Sabbath, and she must return home. But he entreated her not to spoil his pleasure, for he should not enjoy it, unless she went with him; and to please him she consented to go. The boat was upset, and she was drowned. The distracted brother now gave vent to his grief in the most bitter lamentation. He had been the means of her death. There he stood, wringing his hands in agony, and exclaiming, "Oh! what shall I do! How can I see my father's face!"

✺ The young Sabbath-breaker

There was a boy in Boston, the son of respectable parents, who gave promise of becoming a respectable and useful man. He stood well in school, and had the reputation of being a good scholar. He attended the Sabbath school, and appeared to be a good boy. His mother was endeavoring to bring him up in the way he should go. But, on one Sabbath, he was persuaded by some bad boys not to go to Sabbath school, but to go with them to Chelsea. This was his first step in the downhill road. The next thing was, to conceal his conduct from his mother. She asked him if he had been to Sabbath school, and he said he had. Then she asked him for the text. He repeated a text; and as she was not able to go that afternoon, she could not detect his deception. He also pretended to repeat parts of the sermon, in order to blind her eyes. She was satisfied, supposing he had been at Sabbath school and meeting, secure from temptation. Finding he had succeeded so well in deceiving his mother, he continued to seek his pleasure on God's holy day, and to repeat his deceptions to his mother, making her believe that he had been at Sabbath school and meeting. He went on so for some time, hardening himself in sin, and associating with bad boys, till he became ripe for mischief and crime. He was employed by the publisher of a paper, as an errand boy. One part of his duty was to bring letters and papers from the post office. While thus engaged, he learned that money frequently came to his employer in letters.

After a while, he left this employment. The money in the letters now tempted him. Having hardened his heart by breaking the Sabbath, associating with bad boys, and deceiving his mother, he had not strength of principle to resist. He continued to receive the letters, robbing them of their contents. At length he was detected, and sent to prison for two years. The gentleman who related this to me said he went one day to the prison, and there he saw the boy's mother and sister, talking with him through an iron-grated window, and weeping as though they would break their hearts. All this came upon him by his seeking his pleasure on God's holy day. And if you knew the history of those who have been imprisoned for crime, you would find a great many such cases. If he had turned away his foot from the Sabbath, from seeking his pleasure on this holy day, he might have been sitting with his mother and sister in their own quiet home, instead of being locked up in a filthy prison, with a company of hardened criminals.

❧ A melancholy example

Some years ago, a young lady in New York went out on Sabbath morning, as her mother supposed, to go to meeting. Indeed, I believe she told her mother that she was going to church. I think it most likely, from the story as it appeared in the papers at the time, that she started with the intention of going to the house of God. She was seen on the sidewalk, speaking with a young man. It was not known what conversation passed between them; but it was supposed, from what followed, that he was an acquaintance of hers, and was inviting her to an excursion to Hoboken, a place of great resort for pleasure near New York, on the opposite side of the river. Very little is known of the manner in which she spent the day. Probably, they first had a sail for pleasure on the river, and afterwards promenaded the beautiful walks and delightful groves of Hoboken. She was seen, in the afternoon, in company with some young men, at a public house of low character at Hoboken. Her body was found, the next day, at some distance from the house. She had been shamefully abused and murdered.

This melancholy case affords a striking illustration of the single point that I desire strongly to impress on your mind – GOD WILL NOT PROTECT THE SABBATH-BREAKER. When we trample on his holy day, he leaves us to ourselves. And what can we do without his protection? If he forsakes us, who can save us from destruction? This case shows, also, the great danger to which girls or young ladies expose themselves, when they smother the voice of conscience, and consent to go, with a company of Sabbath-breakers, in pursuit of pleasure, on God's holy day. The young man, who has so hardened his heart as openly to trample on the fourth commandment, will not scruple to violate any other of God's commands, when temptation and opportunity present themselves. It was so in this case. The young men in whose company this young lady entrusted herself were a band of Sabbath-breakers. You see what they did in the end. If you consent to put yourself in the power of boys or young men who will violate the Sabbath, and put yourself out of God's protection, by violating it yourself, you cannot expect any better result.

CHAPTER 11

✺ HABITS

Good and bad habits

Besides what I have noticed in several of the foregoing chapters, there are many things of a general nature, which I shall group together under the title of *habits*. A *habit* is what has become easy and natural by frequent repetition. People not unfrequently become much attached to practices, which at first were very unpleasant. You will sometimes see men chewing, smoking, or snuffing *tobacco*, a most filthy and poisonous plant, a little bit of which you could not be persuaded to take into your mouth, it is so nauseous; yet, by long use, people learn to love it. That is a *habit*. So, likewise, you see persons very fond of drinking intoxicating liquors, which to you would be a nauseous medicine; and which are poisonous and destructive to all. It is *practice* which has made these drinks so pleasant. This is a *habit*.

Habits are both *bad* and *good*; and a habit is a very good or a very bad thing, as it is good or bad. Habits are mostly formed in early life; and a habit, once formed, is difficult to be broken; once fixed, it may follow you as long as you live.

I shall specify a few of the bad habits which boys of your age are liable to contract, with their opposite good habits. It is very likely I shall fail to notice many others, equally important; but these may put you upon thinking, and lead you to discover and correct other bad practices.

I. DILATORINESS or TARDINESS. The tardy boy is dilatory about rising in the morning. Although old Chanticleer is pouring his shrill note of warning into his ear, and the birds are filling the air with their merry song, and the morning rays of the sun are peeping stealthily through the half-closed shutter, still he thinks, *"There's time enough yet"*; and instead of starting up with the lark, he lingers and delays, saying with the sluggard, "A little more sleep, Prov. 6:10 a little more slumber, a little more folding of the hands to sleep." At length he rises, in a yawning mood, and proceeds slowly to pull on his clothes, lingering with every article, looking here and there, and stopping every now and then to play, or to amuse himself in gazing about his chamber. And sometimes he stops, half-dressed, to read a story from a piece of an old newspaper. In this and other ways, he amuses himself until the breakfast bell rings, and he is not ready. Perhaps he has been called half a dozen times to "do his chores," and as often answered, *"Well, I'm coming"*; till, wearied with his delay, his mother or sister has done the work that belonged to him, or his father has been called from his room, or the hired man from his work, to do it for him. At length, he makes his appearance at the table after the blessing, when the rest of the family have begun their meal. But, having just emerged from the foul air of his bedroom, he has no appetite for his breakfast, and feels peevish and fretful. A scowl appears upon his brow, and he turns up his nose at the food spread before him, forgetful alike of his obligations to his Heavenly Father for providing, and to his mother for preparing it. Or, if he sometimes gets dressed before breakfast, he is not in season to do his chores, or to complete the lesson which he left unfinished the night before. He hears the breakfast bell, but he is just now engaged, and thinks, *"There's time enough yet – I'll just finish what I've begun"*; and so he is not in season for the table. He has either detained the table till all are impatient of waiting, or else he takes his seat after the rest have commenced eating. In consequence of this loss of time, he is left at the table to finish his breakfast, and his seat is for some time vacant at prayers, when he comes in and disturbs the whole family. Or, if at any time, he gets his seat with the rest, he is dilatory in finding his place, and is never ready to read when his turn comes. This dilatoriness goes on, till the school hour arrives, and he is not ready; or he delays on the way to school, and arrives, perhaps, just after his class have recited. Sabbath morning, when the bell tolls, and the family are starting for meeting, he is roused from a reverie, and has yet to get ready. And so in everything else this dilatory habit follows him. When his father or mother calls him, instead of promptly making his appearance, to serve them, as a dutiful son should do, he answers, *"Yes, in a minute,"* or, *"Yes, I'm going to."* He must dispose of something else first; and before he comes, the service for which he was called has been despatched by someone else. He does not seem to know how to start quick. He is always in a hurry when the time comes to do anything, because he was dilatory in making preparation when he had time. He is always late – always out of time – vexing those that are about him, and injuring himself. He seems to have *started too late.* You would think that he began too late in the beginning – that he was *born too late*, and has never been able to gain the lost time. Everything comes too soon, before he is prepared for it. If he ever becomes a man, and this habit continues, it will always be a source of vexation and disaster to him. If he is a mechanic, he will fail to meet his engagements, and disappoint, vex, and lose his customers. If he is a man of business, he will fail to meet his appointments, and thus lose many a bargain. He will suffer his notes to be protested at the bank, and thus injure his friends and destroy his credit. His dilatory habits will be the ruin of his business. And if he carries the same habit into religion, he will ruin his soul, for *death will overtake him before he is ready.*

Although this seems *natural* to him, it is only tardiness indulged till it has grown into a habit. But by timely resolution, diligence, and perseverance, the habit may be broken.

The opposites of this are the good habits of *promptness and punctuality.* When the gray dawn steals in at his window, the prompt lad springs from his bed; and in a few minutes he is washed and dressed, and on his knees at his morning devotions. Soon he appears at his work; and before breakfast, all his *chores* are done. Thus he has redeemed the time between breakfast and school, which he has at his own disposal, for his lessons or his sports. He is *always in time.* He never keeps the table waiting for him, and never comes after the blessing. He is never late at prayers – never late at school – never late at meeting; and yet he is never in a hurry. He redeems so much time by his promptness, that he has as much as he needs to do everything well and in season. He saves all the time that the dilatory spends in sauntering in considering what to do next, in reading frivolous matters, and in gazing idly at *vacancy.* Do you desire to possess these good habits? Only carry out for one day the idea I have given of promptness, and then repeat it every day, and, in a little time, you have the habit established.

II. SLOVENLINESS.   A slovenly boy makes himself a deal of needless trouble, and greatly tries the patience of his mother. If you go into his room, you find it always in confusion. His things are scattered about, here and there, some on the bed, some on the chairs, and some on the floor – but none in their places. He either has no particular place for anything, or else he takes no pains to put things in their places. He leaves a thing where he uses it. Hence, if he wants anything, he never knows where to look for it, unless he happens to remember where he used it last. He must waste his time in hunting for it. Hence you will often hear him impatiently inquiring if anyone has seen his things; when he ought himself to know where they are. If he goes into another person's room, whatever article he lays his hand upon is misplaced. And so it is, if he uses any of his father's tools. He never thinks of putting anything where he found it. He throws it down carelessly wherever he happens to be, or else puts it in the wrong place; so that, when wanted, it cannot be found. Thus, he not only wastes his own time, but hinders and vexes others. If he goes into the library, and takes down a book, he either puts it in a different place, and so disarranges the shelves, or lays it down on the shelf in front of other books, for his father or mother to arrange. His school books are torn and dirty – disfigured with pencil marks, blots of ink, grease spots, finger prints, and dog's-ears; and if he borrows a book from the Sabbath school library, or of a friend, it is returned with some of these *his marks* upon it.

Whatever he undertakes to do is done in the same slovenly style. If he brings in water, he spills it on the floor. His wood he throws down in a sprawling manner, instead of laying it in a neat and handsome pile. Nothing that he does looks neat and finished.

Nor does he appear to any better advantage in his person. His clothes are put on in a slouching, uncouth manner; and he always contrives to have them dirty. He cannot have on clean clothes half an hour without soiling them. He rubs against whatever dirty thing he passes. If he carries milk, he spills it on his clothes. He drops grease on them at the table. He wallows in the dirt. He contrives to hitch against a nail, or the latch of a door, and makes a rent for his mother to mend. If left to himself, his face would never come in contact with water, nor his teeth with a brush. You would almost think, sometimes, that you could see the grass growing on his upper lip.

He comes into the house with his shoes covered with mud, and never thinks of wiping his feet, but leaves the prints of them on his mother's clean floor or nice carpet. He seems to forget what scrapers and mats are made for, for he passes by without using them. He lays his hat on a chair, or throws it upon the floor, instead of hanging it in its place. Thus he tries the patience of his mother and sisters, and makes himself unwelcome at his own home.

And with this habit is generally associated carelessness. He never seems to be thinking what he is about. He does not see things that are in his way, but stumbles over them, breaking, bruising, or otherwise injuring them, and often hurting himself. You dread to see him approach, lest some mischief should happen. He does not look to see what he steps on, nor whether his hands have firm hold of the article he takes up. If he passes through a door, he does not mind whether it was open or shut; and most likely, if he finds it open, in a warm summer's day, he will close it; but, if he finds it carefully shut, on a freezing day in midwinter, he will leave it wide open.

A careless person will be constantly meeting with accidents and misfortunes, and continually subject to the most vexatious mortifications, which a little thoughtfulness and care would prevent. This habit is a very great fault, and, when confirmed, very difficult to correct. It is therefore the more important, that it should be taken in season, and nipped in the bud.

I need not tell you what are the opposites of slovenly and careless habits. The neat, orderly, and careful boy has an invariable rule – "A PLACE FOR EVERYTHING, AND EVERYTHING IN ITS PLACE." Go into his room at any hour, and you will find everything in order. He can go in the dark, and lay his hand on anything he wants, so that he never runs the risk of setting the house on fire, by carrying a light into his bedroom. He is so much in the habit of putting things in their proper places, that he never thinks of doing otherwise. He never leaves a thing at random, where he happens to be using it; but always puts it where it belongs. When he undresses, every article of his clothing is folded, and laid together in the order that it will be wanted in the morning; so that he loses no time in hunting for it. His clothes are put on and adjusted so as to show a neat fit, and every button does its office. His shoes are regularly brushed every morning, and the strings neatly tied, so that your eye is never offended with the appearance, nor your ear distressed with the sound, of dirty, slipshod, flapping shoes.

To whatever part of the house he goes, he leaves it in the order in which he found it; for it is his invariable rule, when he uses anything belonging to another, to replace it exactly as he found it. When he takes hold of a cup, or a lamp, or any such article, he is careful to get fairly hold, and then to move moderately, and not with a jerk; and by this means, he seldom meets with any of those accidents which are so annoying to tidy housekeepers. If he goes to the library, he is careful to replace every book or paper he takes in his hand, exactly as he found it. If he takes a book to read, he carries it with care, firmly grasped in his hand, and avoids letting it fall, or hitting it against anything to bruise the cover. He holds it in such a manner as not to strain the back or crumple the leaves; and if called away from his reading he puts in a mark, shuts the book, and lays it in a safe place. He never thinks of using a book for any other purpose than that for which it was made. When he has finished reading it, he carefully replaces it in the library, just where he found it. He does not place it wrong end upwards, nor the title towards the back of the shelf; but puts it in the place where it belongs, makes it stand straight, and shoves it back even with its fellows. All his school books are kept neat and clean. No blots of ink, nor pencil marks, nor thumbprints, nor dog's-ears, any where appear. If he passes through a door into or out of a room where others are sitting, he leaves it open or shut as he found it; judging that the persons occupying the room, have adjusted its temperature to their own liking.

He is equally careful of his person. He never considers himself dressed, till he has washed his hands and face, cleaned his teeth, and combed his hair; and he never thinks of sitting down at the table with dirty hands. He learns to keep his clothes neat and clean. At table, he avoids dropping his food upon them. At school, he is careful of his ink, not to bespatter his clothes with it. And at play, he keeps himself out of the dirt. He will wear his clothes a week, and have them appear cleaner, at the end of it, than the sloven's when he has worn them a single day.

He has a care, also, of the appearance of the house. He never forgets to use the scraper at the door, to remove the mud from his feet; and then he makes it an invariable rule never to pass a mat without wiping his shoes. He never says, like the sloven, "I didn't think," to excuse himself. He would consider it unpardonable in him *not to think*; for what is the ability of thinking worth, if it never comes when it is wanted.

The neat, orderly boy, makes himself agreeable to his mother and sisters, who are always glad to see him coming; and home is a delightful place to him, because he meets with smiles and pleasant words. But the sloven exposes himself to sour looks and chiding, by his dirty habits; and he finds home a disagreeable place, because he makes it so.

III. RUDENESS.   This term does not describe any one habit in particular, but a great many little ones. Webster gives the following definition: "RUDE: rough; of coarse manners; unpolished; clownish; rustic." It is not, therefore, a single habit, but a series of habits. These are so numerous, it can hardly be expected that I should think of them all. The rude boy is rough, clownish, and boisterous, in his manners. He is rude in speech and rude in behavior. He will stalk into the house with his hat on; and if there is company, he does not notice them. He talks in a loud and boisterous manner, often breaking in abruptly upon the conversation of others. If he hears part of a conversation, and desires to know what it is about, he abruptly breaks in, "Who is it? Who is it? What is it?" And, often, he keeps his tongue running continually, like the incessant clatter of a mill.

It is rude and vulgar to interlard conversation with *bywords*, or unmeaning phrases, thrown in at random between the sentences. It is much more so, to throw in *little oaths*, or low, vulgar expressions. All this shows a disposition to be profane. It is saying, in effect, "I would swear, if I durst." If indulged, this habit will be very likely to lead on to profaneness.

Another rude habit, which boys often indulge, is, what is familiarly called "CRACKING JOKES" upon one another. The object seems to be, to see who can say the wittiest thing, at another's expense. But, in such attempts, generally, *wit* fails; and the strife is, which can say the silliest thing, in the silliest manner. All such low witticisms may be set down as decidedly rude and vulgar.

Rudeness of behavior manifests itself in so many forms, that it is scarcely definable. I can only glance at a few things which indicate a want of good breeding. It is rude to be so *forward* as to treat your superiors as equals, or to take the lead in all companies. On the other hand, it is rude to be *bashful* – to hang down the head, with a *leer* of the eye, in the presence of company, and refuse to speak when spoken to, or to speak in a confused and mumbling tone, as though you had never seen anybody before. It is rude for a boy to take the best seat in the room, or to take the only seat, while others are standing. Tilting one's chair; sitting awkwardly on one side of the chair, or with the feet stretched out at full length; putting the feet on another's chair; sitting on two chairs; rocking; drumming with the fingers or feet; scratching books, furniture, window frames, or walls – these, and a hundred other things that might be named, are rude habits, which indicate not only the want of good breeding, but the absence of good taste and a sense of propriety.

There are other rude habits, which boys often contract, while abroad, that are wholly out of character for one that would be a *gentleman*; such as hallooing in the streets, jumping on the backside of carriages; calling out to strangers that are passing; collecting in groups about public places, and staring at people. All such behavior is intolerable; and those who are guilty of it will be set down by all sensible people as low, ill-bred, rude boys.

IV. EVIL HABITS.   I am sorry to say that some boys indulge habits, that are worse than any I have mentioned. Boys may be seen strutting through the streets, puffing cigars; and even sometimes filling their mouths with that loathsome Indian weed, *tobacco*, as though they thought such vile habits necessary to make them men. And often you will hear the profane oath issuing from their mouth, along with the foul breath created by this nauseous potion. A disposition to smoke or to chew this filthy, poisonous substance, indicates the existence of an intemperate appetite, and the love of low company. You will, perhaps, see the same boys at the shops, drinking beer. But this is only the prelude to something stronger. Tobacco is one of the most active vegetable poisons. It disorders the system and creates an appetite for stimulants. It is dangerous to use it in any form. But when a boy goes so far as to contract a relish for intoxicating drinks, his ruin is well nigh accomplished. After once giving indulgence to any of these practices, the down-hill road is easy and rapid. About the time when temperance societies began to be formed, I was conversing with a mechanic, who informed me that almost every one of his fellow apprentices, who were in the habit of occasionally drinking intoxicating liquors, had become drunkards. Many years ago, there were, in one of our large cities, fifty young men, clerks in stores, who used to frequent a particular place, to spend their evenings in a social way, with the wine bottle as a companion of their social cheer. One evening, one of them, after retiring, began to reflect upon the consequences of the course he was pursuing. He came to the conclusion, that, if he went on, it would be his ruin. He resolved that he would never go again. The next evening, he found himself on the way to the same place. But as he came to the corner of the street which turned towards the place, he thought of his resolution. He hesitated a moment, and then said to himself, *"Right about face!"* He returned, and was never seen there again. That man is now one of the most wealthy, respected, and useful men in the country; while forty of those who continued their resort to the public house, became intemperate, and I believe have all gone down to the drunkard's grave.

Gaming is another evil habit, which leads to all manner of evil company and evil practices. It has proved the destruction of thousands of promising youth.

Never suffer yourself to become the slave of any habit. Abstain entirely from intoxicating drinks, tobacco, gaming, and profane language. For when you once begin, with any of these, it is like "the letting out of waters." At first they run very slowly; but soon they wear away a channel, and rush on with an impetuosity, which defies all attempts to stop them. On the coast of Norway, there is a great whirlpool, called the *Maelstrom*, which sometimes swallows up great ships. When a vessel comes near this terrible abyss, it is first drawn very gently, with a circular motion. But after it has made one or two rounds, it goes more and more rapidly, and draws nearer and nearer the centre, till finally it reaches the vortex, is swallowed up, and is seen no more. So it is with these bad habits. When one gets fairly within the circle of their influence, his fate is well nigh sealed. The only safety, with young men and boys, is to keep far away from the very outer edges of the whirlpool.

CHAPTER 11

❧ HABITS

Good and bad habits

Besides what I have noticed in several of the foregoing chapters, there are many things of a general nature, which I shall group together under the title of *habits*. A *habit* is what has become easy and natural by frequent repetition. People not unfrequently become much attached to practices, which at first were very unpleasant. You will sometimes see men chewing, smoking, or snuffing *tobacco*, a most filthy and poisonous plant, a little bit of which you could not be persuaded to take into your mouth, it is so nauseous; yet, by long use, people learn to love it. That is a *habit*. So, likewise, you see perse ins very fond of drinking intoxicating liquors, which to you would be a nauseous medicine; and which are poisonous and destructive to all. It is *practice* which has made these drinks so pleasant. This is a *habit*.

Habits are both *bad* and *good*; and a habit is a very good or a very bad thing, as it is good or bad. Habits are mostly formed in early life; and a habit, once formed, is difficult to be broken; once fixed, it may follow you as long as you live.

I shall specify a few of the bad habits which girls of your age sometimes contract, with their opposite good habits. It is very likely

I shall fail to notice many others, equally important; but these may put you upon thinking, and lead you to discover and correct other bad practices.

I. DILATORINESS, or TARDINESS.   The tardy girl is dilatory about rising in the morning. Although old Chanticleer is pouring his shrill note of warning into her ear, and the birds are filling the air with their merry song, and the morning rays of the sun are peeping stealthily through the half-closed shutter, still she thinks, *"There's time enough yet"*; and, instead of starting up with the lark, she lingers and delays. She rises in a yawning mood, and slowly and tardily proceeds to adjust her dress, lingering with every article, perhaps stopping to view it in some point which she had not noticed before; or she casts her eye on a piece of an old newspaper, and stops to read that; or her attention is attracted by something on the wall; she stands a long time at the glass, fixing her hair, or adjusting her curls; and thus the time is frittered away, till the breakfast bell rings, and she is not ready. Her mother and the hired girl have been up an hour and a half; and perhaps she has been called three or four times, and as often answered, *"Well, I'm coming."* At length she makes her appearance at the table after the blessing, when the rest of the family have begun their meal. Or, if she gets dressed before breakfast time, she is not in season to render the assistance to her mother which she needs, or to complete the lesson, which, through her tardiness, she left unfinished the evening before. She hears the bell, but she is just now engaged, and thinks *"There's time enough yet – I'll just finish what I've begun"*; and so she is not in season at the table. She has either detained the table till all are impatient of waiting, or else she takes her seat after the rest have commenced eating. But she is so dilatory in preparing her food, that she is hardly ready to begin till the rest have half finished their meal. She is left at the table to finish her breakfast, and her seat is for some time vacant at prayers, when she comes in and disturbs the whole family. This dilatoriness goes on, till the school hour arrives, and she is not ready. At five or ten minutes past nine, she seizes her satchel, and hastens to school, where she arrives, out of breath, just after her class has recited. On Sabbath morning, when the bell tolls and the family start for meeting, they are detained at the door to wait for her; she has neglected to find her muff, her gloves, or her Sabbath school book, and she must stop and look it up. Thus it is in all things. When her mother calls her, instead of promptly coming to her assistance, it is, *"Yes, in a minute,"* or, *"Yes, I'm going to."* She must dispose of something else first. She does not seem to know how to start quick. She is always in a hurry when the time comes to do anything, because she was dilatory in making preparation when she had time. She is always late – always out of time – vexing those that are about her, and injuring herself. She always seems to have *started too late.* You would think she began too late in the beginning – that she was *born too late*, and so always keeps behindhand. Everything comes *too soon*, before she is prepared for it. She will probably keep her wedding party waiting half an hour after the time set, before she will be ready for the ceremony. It is greatly to be feared that she will carry this dilatory habit into religion, and that *death* will overtake her *before she is ready.*

Although all this seems natural to her, yet it is only tardiness indulged till it has grown into a habit. It has become a sort of *second nature.* But by resolution, diligence, and perseverance, the habit may be broken.

The opposites of this are the good habits of PROMPTNESS AND PUNCTUALITY. The prompt girl will rise with the lark in the morning. When the gray dawn steals in at her window, she springs from her bed, and in a very few minutes, she is dressed, and prepared to make her appearance in the family, to assist her mother, if necessary, or, if not needed there, to go to her devotions and her study. She has done, perhaps, in fifteen or twenty minutes, what the dilatory girl would be an hour and a half in doing, and done it equally well. She is *always in time*. Her promptness enables her to be punctual. She never keeps the table waiting for her, and never comes after the blessing. She is never late at prayers – never late at school – never late at meeting; and yet she is never in a hurry. She redeems so much time by her promptness, that she has as much as she needs to do everything well and in time. She saves all the time that the dilatory spends in sauntering, in considering what to do next, in reading frivolous matters, and in gazing idly at vacancy. Do you desire to possess these good habits? Only carry out the idea I have given of promptness one day, and then repeat it every day, and in a little time you have the habit established.

II. UNTIDINESS. An untidy girl leaves her things scattered about her room. She never has a place for anything; or if she has, she does not keep anything in it. She leaves a thing where she uses it. Her room is all confusion. If she wants anything, she never knows where it is, but must hunt till she finds it, which costs her a great deal more precious time than it would have done to have put it in its proper place. If she goes into another person's room, whatever article she lays her hand upon is misplaced. She never thinks of putting it where she found it; but either throws it carelessly down, or puts it in the wrong place. If she goes to the library, and takes down a book, she either puts it up in a different place, and thus disarranges the shelves, or she lays it down on the shelf in front of other books, for her father or mother to arrange. If she carries a book from the library to read, she leaves it wherever she happens to be when she stops reading; and, perhaps, lays it down open upon its face, soiling its leaves, and straining it out of shape. And the next time she comes that way, if she happens to want to open the window, she will take the same book, without any regard to its value, and put it under the window. By this time, she has let it fall half a dozen times on the floor, bruising its nice binding, and loosening the leaves. And all the while she is reading, her fingers are busily employed in crumpling the leaves. Thus, by the time the book gets back to the library, it is in a worse condition than it would have been in two years with careful handling. Her school books are torn and dirty; disfigured with pencil marks, blots of ink, grease spots, fingerprints, and dog's-ears; and if she borrows a book from the library, or of a friend, it is returned with some of these *her marks* upon it.

If she goes into the kitchen, she is sure to put the tidy house-keeper in a passion, for whatever she lays her hand upon is out of place. Nor does her own person appear to any better advantage. Her dress is adjusted in bad taste; it seems to hang out of shape. You would say her garments were *flung* upon her; and you feel an involuntary anxiety lest they should *fall off*. You do not perceive precisely what is the matter, but there is an evident want of neatness and taste. Her hair wears the same air of negligence; her face often discovers the lack of soap, and her finger nails want attention.

These are only a few examples of the effects of untidy habits. When untidiness becomes a habit, it runs through everything. And the untidy girl will make an untidy woman; and the untidy woman will make an untidy house; and an untidy house will spoil a good husband. A man of taste cannot enjoy himself where everything is out of order; and he will seek that pleasure abroad which he finds not at home.

The twin sister of untidiness is CARELESSNESS. The careless girl is always unfortunate. If she goes into the kitchen, to assist about the work, she splashes water on the wall, drops oil on the floor, spills fat in the fire, scorches her clothes, burns her biscuit, breaks the crockery, or cuts her fingers with the carving knife.

If directed to sweep the family room, she oversets a lamp, or brushes off a table cover, and sends Bibles and hymnbooks sprawling on the floor; or if passing through the parlor, she swings her dress against the centre table, and brushes off the costly books, bruising their fancy binding, and soiling their gilt edges. Every where she goes, something is found in ruins. The trouble is, she *does not think* – she does not *observe*; or else her thoughts and observation are on something besides what is before her. She does not mind what she is doing. She does not look to see what she steps on, nor whether her hands have firm hold of the article which she takes up. If she passes through a door, she does not mind whether it was open or shut; and most likely, if she finds it open in a warm summer's day, she will close it; but if she finds it carefully shut on a freezing day in midwinter, she will leave it wide open.

I need not tell you what are the opposites of these habits. The careful and tidy girl has an invariable rule, that saves her a deal of trouble – "A PLACE FOR EVERYTHING, AND EVERYTHING IN ITS

PLACE." Go into her room at any time, and you will find everything in order. She can go in the dark, and lay her hand on any article she wants; and hence, she never adds to her mother's anxiety, by taking a light to her bedroom. She is so much in the habit of putting things in their proper place, that she never thinks of leaving them any where else. She never leaves a thing at random where she happens to be using it, but always puts it where it belongs. When she undresses, every article of her clothing is folded, and laid together in the order that she will want to take it up in the morning; so that she loses no time in hunting for it. Her dress is adjusted with neatness and taste, every article being in the right place, every button, every hook, every string, every pin, doing its appropriate work, and nothing left loose and dangling, nor hanging in a one-sided manner. To whatever part of the house she goes, she leaves it in the order in which she found it; for it is her invariable rule, when she uses anything belonging to another's department, to replace it exactly as she found it. And when she takes hold of a cup of water, a lamp, or an article of crockery, she is careful to get fairly hold, and then to move moderately, and not with a flirt; and by this means, she seldom spills any liquid or breaks any crockery. If she goes to the library, she is careful to replace every book or paper she takes in her hand, exactly as she found it. If she takes a book to read, she carries it with care, firmly grasped in her hand, and avoids letting it fall, or hitting it against anything to bruise the cover. She holds it in such a manner as not to strain the back, nor crumple the leaves; and if called away from her reading, she puts in a mark, shuts it up, and lays it in a safe place. She would as soon think of using a silver spoon as a book, to put under a window. And when she has finished reading it, she carefully replaces it in the library, just where she found it. She does not place it wrong end upwards, nor the title towards the back of the shelf; but puts it in the place where it belongs, makes it stand straight, and shoves it back even with its fellows. All her school books are kept in a neat and tidy manner. No blots of ink, nor pencil marks, nor thumbprints, nor dog's-ears, any where appear. If she passes through a door, into or out of a room where other persons are sitting, she leaves it open or shut, as she found it, judging that the persons occupying the room have adjusted its temperature to their own liking. The great difference between her and the careless girl is, that she *has her thoughts about her*, while the other *never thinks*. *"I didn't think,"* is the careless girl's excuse; and that excuse is worse than the careless act itself.

III. There is another very uncomfortable habit, which, for the want of a better name, I shall call NOISINESS. It is made up of talkativeness, loud laughing, humming patches of song tunes, and in general, a noisy, bustling activity. *Talkativeness* itself is a very bad habit for a little girl or a young lady. It is a good thing to be sociable, and to converse freely and affably at the proper time, and in the proper place. But there is as much difference between this and talkativeness, as there is between the quiet, purling stream, and the noisy, babbling brook. "The tongue of the wise," says Solomon, _{Prov. 15:2} "useth knowledge aright; but the mouth of fools poureth out foolishness." In the margin it reads, *belcheth*, or *bubbleth*. The thoughts of the heart come belching out like water from a bottle, without regard to sense, order, or arrangement, as though the chief object of the tongue were to make a noise. And one that is always babbling must needs talk nonsense, for want of something sensible to say. A talkative girl will tell all she knows, and all she can remember that she has ever heard anybody say, to everyone she meets. She will take up the time and occupy the attention of others, in relating long, humdrum stories about matters and things which no-body cares to hear. You wait with impatience to hear the end of her story, that you may have a little quiet; but her tongue never stops, but, like the clapper of a mill, keeps up its incessant clack. Such a habit is very disagreeable to others, and makes one appear to great disadvantage. It leads to the constant violation of the principles of good breeding. No one, especially a young lady, who understands what belongs to good manners, will presume on her own impor-tance enough to suppose that others will be pleased to *hear* her talk and noise *all the time*. And no well-bred person will think of obliging others to listen to her against their will. In listening to the talkative girl, I have often felt an involuntary apprehension for the *little member*, which is obliged to perform so much labor. It must be made of stern stuff, or it would wear out, or, at least, grow weary. It is a wonder that it does not take fire from mere friction. It is nec-essary, occasionally, to stop a mill, to let it cool; but the tongues of some people run incessantly, and yet seem to suffer no injury.

But *noise* is not always confined to the tongue. There is a noisy way of doing things, which makes one think that the girl wants to attract notice. We would not be so uncharitable; for we always like to think well of others, and of none more so than a sprightly, active girl. But the thought comes unbidden, when we see one moving about the house, with a noisy step and a wide sweep, making the concussion of the atmosphere itself announce her approach. And we feel an involuntary sense of incongruity, when we see a noisy, bold girl – it is so contrary to the model which we have formed in our minds of the female character.

The opposite of this habit is QUIETNESS. The quiet girl moves about the house with a modest air, and a gentle step, as if fearful al-ways of disturbing others. She involuntarily shrinks from the gaze of others; and, therefore, she does as little as possible to attract notice. She has, indeed, a *tongue*; but she values it too highly to keep it constantly running. Her silence does not run into a prudish reserve. She speaks with grace when spoken to, or when her sense of propriety sees a fitting occasion. But she never speaks for the mere sake of talking, nor unless she has something to say. She is especially careful not to incommode others by her talk, nor to presume on entertaining them with mere *tittle-tattle*. She loves to *sing*; but she remembers that humming *shreds and patches* of old tunes and songs incessantly, besides the want of taste, may incommode others; and therefore she waits for proper opportunities, when she may blend her voice in harmony with others, or exercise herself in this sweet art by herself.

There is nothing which sheds such a soft lustre upon the female character in youth, as gentleness of spirit, and a modest, quiet behavior. These traits of character will always make a favorable impression upon strangers; while it is difficult ever to wear off the unpleasant first impression that is made by a bold, noisy, boisterous girl.

IV. There are several other habits that I shall speak of in connection with other things, and therefore omit them here. I shall only notice one more in this place, and that is RUDENESS. This term does not describe any one particular habit, but a great many little ones. Webster defines it thus: "Rough; of coarse manners; unpolished; clownish; rustic." It is not, therefore, *a habit* merely, but a *series of habits*; and these so numerous, that it can hardly be expected that I should do any more than to give a few specimens, to show what I mean by *rude habits*. These I shall mention at random, as they occur to my mind, without any attempt at order or

arrangement; presuming that the minds of my readers will immediately suggest a great many more, of similar character. Rudeness
manifests itself both in speech and behavior. The habit of interlarding conversation with *bywords*, or unmeaning phrases thrown in
at random, between the sentences, is exceedingly rude, and especially unbecoming in a young lady. If I could write down some con-
versations of this kind, just as they are spoken, I think the practice
would appear so ridiculous, that you would never indulge it. *Bywords*, or *by-phrases*, of whatever kind, add nothing to the force or
beauty of conversation; but some that are in common use among
low-bred people are objectionable, on the score of vulgarity, approaching to profaneness. Such a habit indicates, indeed, a disposition to be profane, restrained only by fear. The use of low expressions, ungrammatical language, and a sort of *chimney-corner
dialect*, is a rude habit, which, if indulged, may cost you great effort
to overcome. If you would be a well-bred lady, never indulge any
habit of this kind; and be particular in your common conversation,
to observe the rules of grammar, and of correct taste, yet without
affectation of preciseness. By beginning in this manner, you will
form the habit of conversing in an easy, pure, and chaste style, free
from all rudeness and vulgarity.

Another rude habit of speech, much practised among the young,
is *coarse jesting* – running upon one another, with the use of low
witticisms upon each other's peculiarities. I do not know that I am
able to describe what I mean, so that you will understand me. I
would give you a specimen, if I could do so without being rude
myself. It is rude and uncivil to seek, even in pleasantry, to wound
the feelings of any.

Rudeness of behavior is almost indefinable. I shall only be able
to mention a few things as specimens – such as tilting one's chair;

sitting awkwardly; sitting on two chairs; putting the feet on another's chair; rocking; drumming with the fingers or feet; scratching books, furniture, window frames, or walls; and a hundred other things that might be named, which indicate not only the want of good breeding, but the want of good taste, and a sense of propriety. I have seen a little miss come into the room where I have been visiting, and, throwing herself into the rocking chair, rock violently back and forth, with as much assurance as if she were amusing herself in a swing. I have seen the same thing in a young woman. But, a little girl, or a young lady, who possessed a nice sense of propriety, would not have presumed, on such an occasion, to seat herself in the rocking chair at all. I once met a young lady, who was attending a boarding school, and during a few moments' conversation in the street, she busied herself in deliberately forming prints with her foot in the mud!

These are but a few specimens of *rude habits*. What I wish to impress upon you, by these examples, is, the necessity of avoiding the formation of habits which indicate rudeness and want of cultivation. All the habits which you form in early life should be such as you will wish to carry with you to the grave; for it is exceedingly difficult to break up a bad habit.

CHAPTER 12

EDUCATION OF THE BODY

Discipline necessary

The reader will perhaps laugh at the idea of *educating* the body. But a moment's reflection will show that no part of man more needs education than the body. The design of education, as I have already said is, to form the character, and prepare us, in early life, for what we are to do in future. For this purpose, the body needs discipline as well as the mind. An ill body makes an ill mind and a sad heart. The health of the body is necessary to the healthy operation of the mind; and a healthy body is secured by activity. But the body not only needs *health*, but discipline. The fingers must be taught all manner of handiwork, and exercised upon it, in order to accustom them to the use that is to be made of them; the feet must be taught to perform their appropriate duties, in a graceful and proper manner; and all the muscles of the body must be exercised, in due proportion, to give them strength and solidity. The proper discipline of the several members of the body is necessary, not only to prepare them for useful occupation, but to give them a graceful, natural, and easy motion, and so promote good manners and a genteel carriage.

I shall not be very particular in what I have to say on this subject, but only give a few gentle hints.

1. DISCIPLINE THE BODY TO OBEY THE WILL. You would not think, to see some young folks, that the will had anything to do with the movements of the body; for it moves in all imaginable ways, with all sorts of contortions. First flies out a foot, then a hand, then there's a twirl or a swing, then a drumming of the fingers, a trotting of the foot, or some such odd figure. This arises from leaving the body to control itself, by its own natural activity, the mind taking no supervision of its motions. Now, if you early accustom yourself to exercise a strict mental supervision over the body, so as never to make any movement whatever, except what you mean to make, you will find this habit of great consequence to you; for, besides saving you the mortification of a thousand ungraceful movements which habit has rendered natural, it will enable you to *control your nerves*, the necessity for which you will understand better hereafter than you do now. Make the *will* the ruling power of your body, so as never to do anything but what you mean to do, and you will never get the reputation of *being nervous*.

2. AVOID LATE HOURS. It would seem hardly necessary to give such a direction to young persons still under the control of their parents. But facts too plainly show that parents do not always sufficiently consider the injurious effects of late hours upon the fair and healthy development of the human frame. And the disposition of young people to seek amusement overcomes, with them, the dictates of prudence. But the practice of sitting up late, and especially of being abroad late at night, is a war upon nature. It interrupts the regular course of things. It turns night into day and day into night. If you would be pale-faced, sickly, nervous, and good for nothing, sit up late at night.

3. RISE EARLY. It is said that, to have a fair skin, rosy cheeks, and a fine complexion, one must wash every morning in summer *in the dew*. Whether there is any virtue in the dew or not, I cannot say; but I have no doubt that such would be the effect of the practice proposed. To rise early, before the atmosphere has become heated with the summer's sun, and walk abroad, snuffing the cool breeze, listening to the music of the feathered tribe, and joining in the sweet harmony of nature, hymning forth praise to the Creator, certainly tends to promote health of body and cheerfulness and serenity of mind; and these will make a blooming countenance, and clothe very plain features with an aspect of beauty. The adding of the *dew wash* will do no harm. If you make a rule of washing in the dew, it will stimulate you to sally forth before the sun has driven it away; and you can find no softer water than the dew.

4. USE PLENTY OF WATER. The body cannot be kept in a healthy state, without frequent bathing. It should be washed all over, with cold water, at least once every day, to promote health and cleanliness. One who has never tried it can have no idea of its invigorating effects; and it seems hardly possible that the human system can keep long in order, while this is neglected. The machinery of a watch, after a while, gets dirty, so that it will not run till it is taken to pieces and cleaned. But the machinery of the human body is vastly more intricate than that of a watch. It is made up of an endless number of parts, of various patterns, some of them of the most delicate texture and exquisite workmanship, but all parts of a great machine that is constantly in motion. And there is provision made for carrying off all the dirt that accumulates on its wheels and bands, in little tubes, which discharge it upon the surface of the skin. But unless frequently washed off, it accumulates,

and stops up the ends of these little tubes, and prevents their dis-
charging, so that the offensive and poisonous matter which they
would carry off is kept in the system. Let this go on a little while,
and it cannot fail to produce disease. Therefore, I say, *use plenty of
water.*

5. TAKE CARE OF YOUR TEETH. The teeth have a very important office to perform in the animal economy – that of preparing
the food for the stomach. What is not done by the teeth must be
done by the digestive organs. Therefore, your health is deeply concerned in the preservation of a good set of teeth. The voice and
the countenance, also, plead with you to take care of your teeth. In
almost all cases, teeth may be saved from decay, if attended to in
time. The best directions I can give for preserving the teeth are, to
clean them every day with a brush, and pick them after every meal
with a pointed quill, so as to remove all the particles of food from
between them, and the tartar that adheres to the surface; cleanliness, as well as the safety of the teeth, requires this. You ought to
have your teeth examined and attended to, by a dentist, once or
twice a year. Keeping them clean preserves them from decay; and
if decay commences, a dentist can stop it, if he can take them in
season.

6. BE ACTIVE. The body was made *for use.* Every part of it is
formed for activity. But anything made for use will suffer injury
to lie still. The human body, especially, if suffered to remain inactive, becomes useless. Activity strengthens the parts. If you would
have more strength, you must use what you have, and it will increase. The right use of your members, also, must be learned by
practice. Much practice is necessary, for instance, to train the fin-

gers to the various uses in which they are to be employed, so as (to use a homely phrase) to make them *handy*. The body, likewise, needs exercise, to keep it in a healthy state. The various parts of its machinery have a great work to do, every day, in turning your food into blood, and sending it a great many thousand times, in a vast number of little streams, to every part of the body. But this machinery will not work, if the body is all the time inactive. It requires *motion*, to give it power. There is nothing, therefore, so bad for it as *laziness*. It is like a dead calm to a windmill, which stops all its machinery.

7. LEARN, AT PROPER TIMES, TO BE STILL.   All nature needs repose. If the human system were always kept in the utmost activity, it would soon wear out. For this reason, God has given us periodical seasons of rest – a part of every day, and one whole day in seven. There are times, also, when it is not proper to be active; as, when you are at your devotions, or at family worship, or in the house of God. So, likewise, at school, or in company, or when you sit down with the family at home, as well as in many other cases, activity is out of place. Your body, therefore, will never be *educated*, till you have obtained such control over it, as to be able, at proper times, to *be still*. And I may say, it is a great accomplishment in a young person, to know just when to be still, and to have self-control enough to be still just at the proper time.

8. BE CAREFUL TO KEEP THE BODY IN ITS NATURAL POSITION. This is necessary, not only to preserve its beauty, but to prevent deformity. Sitting at school, or at any sedentary employment, is liable to produce some unnatural twist or bend of the body. The human form, in its natural position, is a model of beauty. But,

when bad habits turn it out of shape, it offends the eye. Avoid a stooping posture, or an inclination to either side. But sit and stand erect, with the small of the back curved in, the chest thrown forward, the shoulders back, and the head upright. A little attention to these things every day, while the body is growing, and the bones and muscles are in a flexible state, will give your form a beauty and symmetry, which you can never acquire afterwards, if you neglect it at this time of life. And it will do more, a thousand times, to keep you in health, than all the doctor's pillboxes.

9. AVOID TIGHT DRESSING, AS YOU WOULD A BLACK SNAKE. You will, perhaps, smile at this. But if you know anything of the black snake, you will recollect that it assaults not with deadly venom, but winds itself around its victim, stops the circulation of the blood, and, if it reaches high enough, makes a rope of itself, to strangle him. I need not tell you that the effects of tight dressing are similar. Whatever part of the body – whether neck, chest, arms, limbs or feet – is *pinched* with tight covering, is subject to the same strangling process produced by the black snake. It obstructs the free circulation of the blood, and produces a tendency to disease in the part so compressed. If you feel an unpleasant tightness in any part of your dress, *remember the black snake.*

10. DISCIPLINE THE MUSCLES OF THE FACE. You may think this a queer direction; but I assure you it is given with all gravity. If you allow every temper of the heart to find a corresponding expression in the muscles of the face, you will be sure to spoil the fairest countenance. How would you feel, if you were to see an accomplished young person, with fine features, and a beautiful countenance; but on coming near, should discover little holes in the face,

from which, every now and then, vipers and venomous serpents were thrusting out their heads and hissing at you? Well, the evil tempers of the heart, such as pride, vanity, envy, jealousy, etc., are a nest of vipers; and, when indulged, they will spit out their venom through the countenance. How often do we see a proud, scornful, sour, morose, or jealous expression, that has fairly been worn into the features of the countenance! And what is this but the hissing of vipers that dwell within? Strive to acquire such self-control, as to keep a calm, serene expression upon your countenance; and you cannot tell how much it will add to your appearance.

11. BE TEMPERATE.   To be strictly temperate is, to *avoid all excess*. Not only abstain from eating and drinking what is hurtful, but use moderation in all things – in eating and drinking, in running and walking, in play, in amusement.

CHAPTER 13

✿ ON USEFUL LABOR

Dislike of work

I have seen boys who would make incredible exertion to accomplish anything which they undertook for their own amusement; but who, when called upon to do anything useful, would demur and complain, put on sour looks, and conjure up a multitude of objections, making the thing to be done like lifting a mountain. Whenever any *work* is to be done, "there is a lion in the way"; and Prov. 26:13 the objections they make, and the difficulties they interpose, make you feel as if you would rather do it a dozen times yourself, than to ask them to lift a little finger. The real difficulty is in the boy's own mind. He has no idea of being useful; no thought of doing anything but to seek his own pleasure; and he is mean enough to look on and see his father and mother toil and wear themselves out to bring him up in idleness. Play, play, play, from morning till night is all his ambition. Now, I do not object to his *playing*; but what I would find fault with is that he should wish to *play all the time*. I would not have him work all the time, for

"All work and no play makes Jack a dull boy";

neither would I have him play all the time, for

"All play and no work makes Jack a *mere toy.*"

There is not a spark of *manliness* in such a boy; and he never will be a man, till he alters his notions.

The coward

There is another boy, who has more heart – a better disposition. When called to do anything, he is always ready and willing. His heart dilates at the thought of helping his father or his mother – of being useful. He takes hold with alacrity. You would think the work he is set about would be despatched in a trice. But he is *chicken-hearted.* Instead of conquering his work, he suffers his work to conquer him. He works briskly for a few minutes, and then he begins to flag. Instead of working away, with steady perseverance, he stops every minute or two, and looks at his work, and wishes it were done. But wishing is not working; and his work does not get done in this way. The more he gazes at it, the more like a mountain it appears. At length, he sits down to rest; and finally, after having suffered more from the dread of exertion than it would have cost him to do his work a dozen times, he gives it up, and goes to his father or mother, and in a desponding tone and with a sheepish look, he says, *"I can't do it!"* He is a *coward.* He has suffered himself to be *conquered* by a woodpile which he was told to saw, or by a few weeds in the garden that he was required to dig up. He will never make a man, till he gets courage enough to face his work with resolution, and to finish it with a *manly perseverance.* *"I can't,"* never made a man.

Do-nothing habits

Here is another boy, who has got the notion into his head that he is going to live without work. His father is rich; or he intends to be a professional man, or a merchant; and he thinks it of no use for him to learn to work. He feels above labor. He means to be a *gentleman*. But he is very much mistaken as to what constitutes a gentleman. He has altogether erroneous and false views of things. Whatever may be his situation in life, labor is necessary to exercise and develop the muscular powers of his body. If he grows up in indolence, he will be weak and effeminate, never possessing the vigor of a man. And whatever sphere of life he may occupy hereafter, he will never possess independence and energy of character enough to accomplish anything. A man who does not know how to work, is not more than half a man. He is so dependent upon others, that he can accomplish nothing without help. Nor can wealth, or education, or professional knowledge, supply the deficiency. Wealth is very uncertain. "Riches take to themselves wings"; and they are Prov. 23:5 especially liable to fly away from men who have been bred up in idle, *do-nothing* habits. And what will they do when their wealth is gone? They have never made any exertion, or depended on themselves. They have no energy of character. They have no knowledge of any useful employment. They cannot dig, and to beg they are ashamed. They either sink down, in utter discouragement, to the lowest depths of poverty, or else they resort to dishonest means of obtaining money. I have before me a letter, written to a gentleman in Boston, from a boy in the *House of Correction*, who got there by trying to live without work. After telling how bad he felt to be shut up in prison, and how bitter his reflections upon his past life were, he says, "I thought that *as long as I could live without work*, and get my living dishonestly, I would *go ahead*; but my high life was soon stopped." Here you perceive that his temptation to be dishonest arose from his dislike of work. But now, he says, he is convinced that the best way to get a living is by *honest labor*. And so you will find it. There is no one more exposed to temptation than the idle boy.

"Satan finds some mischief still
For idle hands to do."

One who undertakes to get a living without work will be very likely to fall into dishonest practices, and get shut up in prison.

Equally necessary is it for a man of learning, or a professional man, to know how to do with his own hands the most common things. If dependent on his own earnings for a support, he will not be able to hire everything done to his hand; or, if able, he will not always find anyone to do it. And as to the merchant, his life, from the very first, is a life of incessant toil and labor. The lazy boy, who goes into a store as a clerk, with such notions in his head about work, will be served as the working bees serve their *drones* – he will be *dragged out of the hive*.

Results of sloth

The boy that despises work, sets himself against nature; and if he succeeds in making anything of himself, he will contradict the voice of all history. When man fell from his innocency, it was determined that he should eat his bread in the sweat of his brow. It is in vain for his posterity to attempt to evade this curse. If they refuse to toil, they will suffer a worse disaster, as the penalty of their disobedience Disease, or poverty, or both, will follow the lazy track of the sluggard. This result, Solomon has described, in the most glowing terms: "I went by the field of the slothful, and by the vineyard of the man void of understanding; and lo, it was all grown over with thorns; nettles had covered the face thereof, and the stone wall thereof was broken down. Yet a little sleep, a little slumber, a little folding of the hands to sleep; so shall thy poverty come as one that travaileth, and thy want as an armed man." [Prov. 24: 30–31, 33–34]

Labor honorable

Many of the ancient nations used to have a law requiring every young man to have a knowledge of some branch of labor. There appears to have been such a custom among the Jews. Paul, though belonging to a wealthy family, and bred a lawyer, in the highest school in the nation, was yet brought up to a trade. And when he came to devote himself to his Master's service, he found his tent-maker's trade of great use to him. And whatever occupation you design to follow, you will find use for all the practical knowledge of *work*, of *handicraft*, or of *mechanical skill*, you can acquire in early life.

In the empire of China, labor is held in such esteem, that the emperor, on the day of his coronation, is required to plough a furrow with his own hand. And if you look over the page of history, both ancient and modern, you will find that many of the greatest men that ever lived, were accustomed to follow some laborious occupation. David, the poet king, the sweet singer of Israel, whose name has been embalmed in the hearts of the pious in all ages, when a boy, was occupied in keeping his father's sheep. Dr. Franklin was the son of a mechanic in Boston, and was bred a printer. Washington, the father of his country, was a farmer. And the blessed Savior himself has set an example of industry and love of labor, which should put to shame every *pseudo-gentleman* who despises the labor of the hands. His apostles, also, were called from laborious occupations to preach the gospel; and many of the most eminent of his ministers and missionaries of the present day have been called from the plough or the workshop; and some of them have *worked their way* through a long course of study, bearing the expenses of their education with the labor of their hands.

We may safely conclude, then, that, whoever despises labor is a fool; for he despises the only thing that can make him A MAN.

Effects of idleness

But industry is not only necessary to *make you a man*; it is necessary to *make you happy*. Some boys have such an aversion to labor, that they would think themselves perfectly happy if they had *nothing to do*. But they are greatly mistaken. They might like such a life a day or two, but they would soon get tired of it. The children at the Sandwich Islands have nothing to do. Their parents have no employment for them. They grow up in idleness. A missionary, writing to the children of this country, says, "Now, does anyone say, 'Happy, happy children, inhabiting these sunny isles! Absolutely nothing to do, but to seek their own gratification, without fear or restraint!' Happy? No. The goats which graze the sides of their mountains may be happy; or the kitten which gambols on your kitchen hearth may be happy; but these children are not happy." They often go hungry. Their parents were brought up in idleness, also; and now they will not work if they can help it. They receive no assistance from their children, and often have no food to give them. The children frequently live upon roots, which they dig in the mountains, or upon sugarcane, which they find in the fields. After spending the day in idleness, they often have to go supperless to bed.

In many parts of the islands, also, the children, who have no disposition to labor and obtain clothing, suffer much from cold. They go almost naked; and when night comes, they lie down on a bare mat, with the dogs and fleas. Would the children of America exchange their warm beds and sweet sleep, for the leisure and hard fare of these young Sandwich Islanders?

But in sickness, their sufferings are much greater. They are destitute of nearly every comfort; they have no physician; and they receive very little attention from their parents and friends. No kind mother watches over their couch at night. If they suffer, they suffer alone; if they die, they die unattended.

Idleness, also, makes these children vicious. Having nothing useful to do, they are always ready for every evil work. They tempt each other to sin. They rush together the downward road; and if spared to become men, they are poor and degraded, diseased and miserable.

But perhaps you will say, "These Sandwich Islanders are uncivilized heathen; and this is what makes them so wretched." But you need not go to heathen lands, to see the bad effects of the want of useful employment, upon boys and young men. In the Southern States, all the labor is done by slaves. It is esteemed disgraceful for a white man to work. The consequence is, that the boys grow up in idleness and vice. They learn everything that is bad. They grow up with strong and fiery passions, and vicious inclinations unsubdued. Among the young men, gambling, horse racing, and other

social vices, generally prevail. But many of them become poor; and
then they are as wretched as the poor Sandwich Islanders. There is,
perhaps, no class of persons, in this country, more degraded than
the poor whites in the slave states. And their poverty and wretchedness may be traced to the fact, that it is disgraceful, among them,
for white men to labor.

Effects of industry

There is no country on earth where there is less of squalid poverty,
and where the people generally enjoy more comfort and happiness,
than in New England. And what is the reason? There is, probably,
no other country in the world where the people are so industrious
– where *all the people* are engaged in some useful employment. In
New England, boys are set to work as soon as they are old enough
to handle a hoe, an axe, or a spade. Every child has something to do,
which adds something to the family's comfort. And where, in the
wide world, will you find so many smiling, happy faces as among
the children of New England? This is the true reason why they are
so much happier than the children of the Sandwich Islands. The
Yankee boy may sometimes get tired of his work; but if he had
nothing to do, he would be absolutely miserable. It is not in the
nature of a son of New England to be happy without employment.
And, where you find one of them educated, and rising to eminence
in professional life, if you trace back his history, in most cases, you
will learn that, when a boy, he worked on his father's farm, or in
his father's shop. And if you could see him seeking relaxation and
amusement, you would often find him engaged in the same kind
of labor that he used to perform when a boy.

When one of the convicts in the state prison has committed an
offence, they punish him by shutting him up in his cell alone, and

giving him nothing to do. For a little while he is glad to be relieved from his work; but very soon, he begs for it again. Nothing is so hard for him to bear as *doing nothing.*

If, then, you would be virtuous and happy – if you would be qualified to brave the storms of life's troubled ocean – *cultivate the love of useful labor.* This will give you independence of character. It will give you the ability to take care of yourself. It will make you despise the fawning sycophant, who would sell his birthright for a piece of bread. It will save you from the temptation to surrender your independence, or commit any act of meanness or dishonesty for the sake of a living.

CHAPTER 13

KNOWLEDGE OF

HOUSEHOLD AFFAIRS

Disdain of work

It is in acquiring a knowledge of household affairs, chiefly, that your body is to be educated. Young girls often have wrong notions about this matter, looking upon *housework* as mere drudgery, only fit for servants. And, especially, if they get it into their heads that they are to be trained up for ladies, they learn to despise all useful labor. And sometimes they become so heartless and unfeeling as to be willing to see their mothers working like slaves, while they set up for ladies. But this is anything but ladylike. The term *lady* was originally applied to a woman of rank, as that of *lord* was to a man of rank. In the old country, society is divided into different orders, the *nobility* and the *common people*. But it is not so among us. Every woman can be a lady, who conducts herself in a ladylike manner. And the true idea of a lady is, a strict propriety of conduct on all occasions. One may, therefore, be a lady as well in the kitchen as in the parlor.

Mrs. Bradish

Nothing will make a woman appear more ridiculous than a contempt for useful occupation, and especially for household affairs. No woman that has the charge of a family can carry out the true idea of a lady, without a knowledge of household duties. She cannot have things done to her mind, nor save herself from the severest mortification, without it. The following well-told story, which I have met with in an old paper, will give a fine illustration of what I mean:

~

It is the middle of January. Business is brisk, and winter parties are frequent. At half past eight o'clock in the morning, a girl stands at the foot of Mrs. Bradish's broad stairs, ringing the bell for breakfast. She returns into the back parlor, and after walking and fidgeting about for a while, begins talking to herself: "I wish Mrs. Bradish would ever come to her meals when the bell rings. She stays half an hour, and then scolds because everything is cold. I'm sure it isn't my fault; there was full an hour and a quarter between the two bells this morning; but she's just as likely to be in time when I allow only fifteen minutes. I'm determined I won't get up so early another morning, that's poz—" She was interrupted by Mr. Bradish's appearance, in morning gown and slippers.

"Why, Bridget, why did you not ring a first bell? Here it is half past eight o'clock; just the hour I promised to meet a western merchant at my store. I shall lose a thousand dollars."

"I did ring a first bell, sir."

"Not at the regular hour."

"We can't have no regular hours, sir. Sometimes the cook isn't up till eight o'clock, and we can't have no fire in the kitchen. And sometimes Mrs. Bradish isn't ready for her breakfast till nine o'clock; and she doesn't like it, if it's cold."

"But I must have my breakfast at eight o'clock. Come, hurry – give me a cup of coffee. This egg is as hard as a stone, and as cold as an icicle. Bring me some hot cakes."

The cakes were brought. "These cakes are sour; they are not fit to be eaten. What is the reason we always have sour cakes?"

"I don't know. The last cook used to put in some white stuff to sweeten them, but I don't think this one knows. She don't seem to know much about cooking."

"It must be soda, or pearlash. Go to her, and tell her to put some into her batter. Run up first, and ask Mrs. Bradish to come down to her breakfast."

Mrs. Bradish and the remodeled cakes made their appearance at about the same time. The former looked dull, listless, and sleepy, with a stray lock of uncombed hair hanging down from beneath a tumbled cap. The latter – that is the cakes – were of a dark sea-green color, and sent forth an odor very much resembling that from a soap boiler's vat. Mr. Bradish swallowed one mouthful; but, on taking a second, he was obliged to walk hastily to the window, where he threw something into the back yard. He returned to the table, making very wry faces.

"Bridget, bring me a cracker, if there is one in the house. My dear, don't eat that bread or those cakes; you will be poisoned. I took a whole mouthful of pure saleratus just now. How I wish we could ever have a pleasant breakfast together, with things hot, and nice, and well-cooked."

"I'm sure it is not my fault; I tell the cook to make them nice."

"Suppose, my dear, you were, for one or two mornings, to get up early, and go into the kitchen to see that things were properly prepared."

"How can I get up early, when I am out, almost every night, till one or two o'clock?"

"Let us go to fewer parties, my dear, and not stay so late when we do go. I should be much happier, and my business would be much better attended to. I think our servants need overseeing."

"Very well, Mr. Bradish. If you wish me to spend my time cooking, and overseeing servants, you should have told me so at first, that I might have learned how. My hands will look pretty in the evening, with the nails all filled with pie crust. And how can I dance the Polka with any spirit, if I'm to be dancing from the kitchen to the parlor all day?"

Just at that moment, there was a heavy thump and a loud squall overhead. "There, that careless little Jane has dropped the baby on the floor. I hope she has not broken any of its bones."

Charles Bradish really loved his wife and child. He followed her upstairs, but seeing the baby was not seriously hurt, he kissed them both, and hurried away. Just as he left the room, he said, "My old friend, Horatio Snelling, is in town. If I see him today, I must ask him home to dinner; and, pray, my dear, be punctual, and have things nice and well served. He is one of my best customers, and he has a capital wife at home."

"I do wonder," said Mrs. Bradish, "what Charles must be bringing people home to dinner for. It is a perfect bore. And how in the world a nice dinner is to be got with a cook just out of an Irish bog, is more than I can tell. It is really a reasonable, pretty thing, to expect me to spend half of my time in the kitchen, teaching and coaxing those that ought to know their business before they come to me!"

At eleven o'clock, however, she went into the kitchen. The marketing had just come – a turkey, a leg of mutton, and a fine fresh fish. "Well, Biddy, I suppose you know how to cook these things. The turkey must be roasted, with a brown gravy made of the giblets. The leg of mutton boiled with caper sauce; the fish must also be boiled and garnished with eggs. Make an apple pie, and some custards; that will be quite sufficient for a second course. And be sure, Biddy, to have it all hot and ready for the table at exactly half past three o'clock."

Biddy said she knew perfectly well how it should be done, and that it should all be ready at the moment.

Mrs. Bradish dressed, and went out to order a new headdress for the evening party. She met a friend who wished her to go shopping; and time slipped away so fast in this manner, that it was three o'clock when she came in. She ran to the kitchen to see what state the dinner was in. The turkey was browning very nicely before a hot fire; and the cook assured her that the mutton and the fish were doing very well. The pies were yet in the oven, but the custards were of such a dingy color, and so burnt upon the outside of the cups, that Susan saw they would not answer to be placed upon the table. "I can make a tipsy cake; Charles likes it, and it will look very well." She sent the girl to the nearest confectioner's, for a sponge cake, while she beat up cream, sugar, and spices. The cake was brought.

"Now run upstairs, and bring down a bottle of wine or brandy, from the dining room closet."

The bottle was brought, and part of the contents poured into a dish. The cake was then laid carefully in, and the custard poured around it. "There, that looks nicely; and how quickly it was done! I did it all myself, too." Saying which, she ran upstairs to change her dress for dinner.

She did not get down in time to receive her husband's friend; but just as she reached the parlor door, the bell rang for dinner, so they passed at once to the dining room. The meats were all on the table; but it looked bare, for a dish of potatoes, boiled with the skins on, was the only vegetable. The waiter girl was sent in haste for some currant jelly, and the fish was uncovered. It was in pieces or flakes, and of a pale brown color. It was garnished with eggs, one of which was streaked with green, and which sent forth such a peculiar odor, that the dish had to be sent out at once from the table. "This turkey looks well," said Mr. Bradish; "but I fear it is not done," continued he, as the passage of the knife disclosed the raw, pink-colored meat. No, the turkey had been too suddenly cooked; there was not a bit even of the bread that was eatable. Susan looked in despair; but her husband, seeing her mortification, tried to put a good face upon the matter. "Well, we must dine upon mutton; and there have been worse things eaten than a good leg of boiled mutton."

Mr. Snelling declared it was his favorite dish.

"But how is this?" exclaimed Mr. Bradish, at the first mouthful; "it tastes of fish more than mutton. It must have been boiled with the fish."

There are certain flavors whose union is pleasant; but mutton and fish do not happen to be of that kind. Mr. Snelling, however, was good-natured and polite. He peeled a potato, helped himself to currant jelly, and appeared to eat with infinite relish, telling all the laughable anecdotes he could think of, about the bulls and mistakes of both foreigners and natives. Neither Charles nor his wife,

however, could converse with any spirit; and they both looked relieved, when the dishes were taken away. Susan hoped that the apple pie would prove eatable; but she was mistaken – the crust was
hard and leathery, and the apples half baked and ill-flavored. The
custard cake was her last and only hope. "Let me help you to some
of this, Mr. Snelling," said she, filling a plate full. "I flatter myself you
will find it good, for I made it myself. Our dinner has proved so very
poor, I hope you will eat heartily of it."

Charles brightened up. He looked at his friend, hoping to hear
him praise his wife's cookery. His guest had a spoonful of the liquid cake in his mouth. His face flushed, his teeth were set together,
while a peculiar heaving motion of the chest showed anything but a
gratified palate. At last, with a tremendous effort, he swallowed it.

"What is it?" said Charles, looking aghast, and at the same time
tasting the dish before him. "Heavens and earth! It is saturated with
nauseous drugs! This is not wine; it is elixir pro!" It was true; the girl,
in her hurry, had mistaken the bottle.

The friend was a humorist, and the whole affair of the dinner,
Mrs. Bradish's chop-fallen countenance, and her husband's rueful
looks, struck him all at once so ludicrously, that he could not refrain
from laughing long and heartily. Few people could resist that laugh,
and Charles was finally obliged to join; but his wife had been too
much mortified, and was now too angry, to partake in their merri-
ment; so she betook herself to her nursery.

~

If Mrs. Bradish had been in the habit of working in the kitchen,
when she was a girl, and if her mother had made it an important
part of her education to learn household affairs, she would never
have suffered these mortifications.

Would-be ladies

Some would-be ladies affect great contempt for labor, and especially scorn to put their hands to any household work. They are afraid of soiling their hands, or of having it known among their fashionable friends that they are in the habit of doing anything *useful*. But such ladies are always unhappy; because they are obliged to be dependent on servants, and they can never get those who will do work to suit them, unless they know how to do it themselves, and are able to give instruction to those whom they employ. They are, likewise, despised by all sensible people; for the greatest merit anyone can have, in the estimation of the people of this country, is, *to be useful*. But a lady who does not know how to take care of herself and of her own house, or who feels above it, cannot be very useful. She will, most likely, be a *laughingstock* among the people. The greater portion of the women of this country, with the assistance of their daughters, do their own work; and some of the most accomplished ladies I have ever seen are not ashamed, when there is occasion for it, to go into the kitchen and cook a meal of victuals. And why should they be? Christian ladies are called by the apostle Peter the daughters of Sarah; and she cooked a supper with her own hands for the angels that came to visit Abraham. King Solomon represents his virtuous woman as seeking wool and flax, and working willingly with her hands, and as rising early and giving meat to her household. No one need be ashamed to be seen engaged in any useful employment; but it is a great shame for any woman who has charge of a house, not to understand how to do what is necessary to manage a house. There is much to interest the mind in household affairs. You may apply your philosophy to sweeping and dusting, and making beds, and find interesting illustrations of what you learn from books in all the arrangements of the house; and in cooking and washing you will find abundance of interesting experiments in chemistry. Yet there are multitudes who would prefer spending their time at fancy needlework, though there is very little required in performing it but mechanical skill. This I do not condemn; but the useful should be set foremost. All ornamental branches of education are to be encouraged; but they will not make amends for the want of skill to cook a meal of victuals, make a plain garment, or darn a stocking. There is more science in boiling a potato, or raising bread, and more judgment required, than there is in executing the finest piece of embroidery. Should you ever become the mistress of a house, your ornamental work will please the sight; but it will never set off against heavy bread and hard, watery potatoes.

CHAPTER 14

EDUCATION OF THE HEART

Moral faculties

By the *heart*, I mean the *moral faculties*, in distinction from the *intellectual*. Any action is *moral*, which can be *praised* or *blamed*. The *moral faculties* are those which determine moral action. These faculties are, the *Conscience*, *Will*, and *Affections*. In this division, I do not attempt metaphysical exactness, but only what I can make my readers understand. When I speak of *educating* these faculties, I do not mean to separate the process from that of religious education in general; for nothing can be well done, in the formation of character, without religious principle and motives at the foundation. But my object is, to speak of the specific means by which these faculties may be cultivated.

It may be necessary for me to explain what I mean by the *Conscience*, *Will*, and *Affections*. Yet it does not fall in with my design, neither would it suit the age and capacities of those for whom I write, to enter into a philosophical description, or analysis, of the faculties of the mind, or affections of the heart. I shall only give such simple explanations as are sufficient for my purpose, and as I suppose will be understood by my readers.

I. The Conscience. This is the faculty which determines whether any action proposed to the mind, or any feeling of the heart, is *right* or *wrong*. If you will watch the motions of your own mind, you will perceive, whenever anything is proposed to be done or not to be done, something within tells you that it is either *right* or *wrong*; if *wrong*, you find the same *something within*, urging you *not to do* it; or, if *right*, the same impulse moves you *to do* it. If you do as you are thus urged, you find the same voice within *approving* what you have done, or, if you do not obey, *condemning* you. This *something within* is CONSCIENCE.

You have, doubtless, lived long enough to experience many a conflict, or dispute, between your *conscience* and your *inclinations*. You are inclined to do something which your conscience tells you is wrong; but conscience not only tella you it is wrong, but urges you not to do it. Your inclinations, or desires, urge you in the contrary direction; and this creates a conflict. If conscience prevails, then it approves your decision, and you feel happy. But, if inclination prevails, conscience upbraids, and you feel miserable.

As I have defined education, you will see the great importance of *educating the conscience*. It is the leading moral faculty, and must have a great influence upon the moral character. For the conscience itself may be wrong. It is not itself the rule by which you are to determine what is right and wrong. The Word of God is the rule. The office of conscience is, to determine whether anything you propose to do is agreeable to the rule, and to urge you, accordingly, to do it or not to do it. Suppose you wish to determine whether anything is straight; you lay a rule upon it that you suppose to be straight, and if they agree, that settles the matter. Your eye, comparing the object with the rule, determines whether it is straight or not. But, if the rule applied is crooked, your eye is deceived, and you misjudge. Conscience is the eye of the soul, that compares an action with the rule. The conscience, then, must be well instructed. You must learn the *rule of right* from the Word of God, and then conscience will always decide right. But, if you adopt false notions of right and wrong, your very conscience will lead you astray. The first thing, then, in the education of the heart is, to have it filled with *right principles*; and these you are to obtain from the study of the Bible, and from listening to the instructions of your parents, teachers, and ministers.

The next thing is, *always to obey the voice of conscience*. If you go contrary to it, and do what conscience tells you is wrong, or neglect what it urges upon you as duty, you weaken that faculty, and harden the heart. When you refuse to hearken to the voice of conscience, the next time it will not speak so loud; and every time this is repeated, the weaker it grows, till at length it is scarcely heard at all, and you may go on and sin almost without restraint. If you will look back a little while in your own experience, you will see the force of what I say. If you have ever fallen into the habit of secretly disobeying your parents, you will find an illustration of it. The first time you were tempted to disobey, your conscience was very loud against it; but the temptation, falling in with your inclinations, prevailed. Then conscience upbraided you with a voice of terror. But you were not discovered, and no immediate evil followed. The next time the temptation presented itself, the remonstrance of conscience was feeble, and its condemnation light. The next time it was feebler still; till at length you could do with careless indifference what at first made you shudder. But when the power of conscience is gone, there is but one step more to ruin. If, then, you would keep your conscience tender, you must always obey its voice.

Another means of educating the conscience is, the habit of thinking with approbation of what is right, and putting out of the mind with horror all thoughts of what is wrong. The most hateful things, by becoming familiar to the sight, lose much of the horror which they excite at first. A person who had never seen an animal killed would be deeply affected at the sight; but a butcher thinks nothing of it. So, by thinking much of what is wrong, the conscience becomes defiled, and ceases to act with promptness and decision; while, if kept familiar only with the good, it would revolt instantly from the bad.

II. The Will.   This is the faculty that *chooses* or *refuses*. It is the *decisive* faculty. It is the power that determines action, whether good or bad. It is the *ruling* faculty of the soul. I said *conscience* was the *leading* faculty, because it goes before the action of the will, and moves it to choose what is right. The *will* is the *ruling* faculty, because it determines all action. The way to *educate the will* is, to accustom it to submit to the dictates of conscience. The will, in our fallen and depraved state, is turbulent and unsubmissive. It is not disposed to submit to the law of God, nor to those whom God has set over us. Yet there is nothing of more importance to our happiness and usefulness than the early subjection of the will. If you determine that you will always have your own will, you will certainly be unhappy; for it is impossible that you should always have your own way. But if you early accustom yourself to give up your own will; to submit to the will of God, as made known to you in his word and Providence – to submit to your parents, as those whom God has set over you, and to your own conscience, as the faithful monitor which God has placed in your own bosom – then you will be as happy as you can be in this imperfect state. This you will not accomplish all at once. It must be the result of experience, trial, and discipline, with the grace of God in your heart. But if you begin to cultivate the *habit of submission*, in early life, it will save you many a severe struggle and much unhappiness. You have doubtless learned, before this time, that you always get into difficulty at home, when you set out to have your own will. And perhaps you have sometimes, in your impatience at contradiction secretly wished that you were of age, beyond the control of your parents, that you might do as you pleased. But I assure you, both from my own experience and from what I have seen of the world, that you will not find it any easier to have your own will, after you come to act for yourself. You will not succeed in anything you undertake to do for others, unless you give up your own will; neither will you succeed in making society agreeable to yourself. Suppose you go to a shoemaker, to get a pair of shoes made, and as soon as you begin to tell him how you wish them done, he answers, "I understand my business; if you want a pair of shoes, I'll make them for you, but nobody can teach me how to do my work?" You would say, "He is a surly creature; I'll have nothing to do with him." Or, suppose you go into company, and you find a young lady who will consent to nothing except what she herself proposes; you say, "She is a selfish creature; let her enjoy herself alone." But all this comes from mere willfulness. You never will be comfortable, much less happy, till you are willing to yield to others, when no principle is concerned, but only the mere gratification of your own will. And when one is employed by another, it is perfectly reasonable that he should be directed by his employer, even if what he is directed to do may appear to him unwise. The only way that you can succeed, and be happy, in anything you may undertake to do for others, is, to submit your will to theirs, and do cheerfully, and without objection, what they require – provided, only, that they do not require you to do wrong. If you will look back, you will find that this *willfulness* has been the cause of all the trouble you have got into with your parents, and of nearly all the altercations you have had with your brothers, sisters, and companions. And, if you retain this disposition, it will make you miserable, whatever station in society you may occupy.

A little boy, named Truman, lost his own mother; and when he was four or five years of age, his father married again. His new mother was an excellent lady, very affectionate and kindhearted toward the children. But one day, when she was teaching Truman how to read, she could not make him say his lesson correctly. She therefore used the rod till he submitted, and read as he ought. He was afterwards overheard talking with himself, about his conduct: "Tru, what made you treat your dear mother so? Hasn't she always been kind to you?" "Yes, I know she has. She loves me, and tries to do me all the good she can." "Then how could you be so naughty, to treat her so?" "I know I have been a very naughty boy, and treated her very bad indeed when she has been very kind to me; and she was trying then to teach me for my own good." "What can you say for yourself, then? How did you come to behave so?" "I can't say anything for myself; I know it was very mean. I feel ashamed to think I could treat her so; and I'll never do it again as long as I live. But I thought I would just try for once, and *see who was master.*"

The object of this little boy was to have his own will. He was not willing to submit to his mother, till he had tried his strength, to see whose will should prevail. He got a severe chastisement, and had to submit after all. And so it will always be with you, if you set out with the determination, if possible, always to have your own will. You will be always getting into difficulty, and gain nothing by it in the end.

III. THE AFFECTIONS.   I shall not undertake in this place, to give a full and complete definition of the affections. It will answer my present purpose, to say that the *affections* are the *feelings* or *emotions of the heart*. This may not be philosophically accurate; but when my readers come, at a more advanced age, to study mental and moral philosophy, they can enlarge their views. For all practical purposes, this will answer. And what I mean by *educating the affections* is, to acquire the habit of controlling the feelings, so as to suppress the bad and cultivate the good. You hear people talk of good and bad *dispositions*. But a good disposition is only the preponderance of good feelings; or in other words, where good feelings and good tempers prevail, we say that person has a good disposition; but if bad feelings and evil tempers predominate, we say he has a bad disposition. There is no doubt a difference in natural dispositions. But with suitable efforts, and especially with the aid of God's grace, much may be done to cultivate and improve them.

~

With these preliminary remarks, I proceed to give some *rules for the cultivation* of the affections.

1. CHECK THE FIRST RISINGS OF ILL TEMPER.   The smith, who makes an edged tool – an axe, a knife, or any such instrument – first works the iron and steel into the form which he wishes, and then *tempers* it. While he is working it, he wants to keep it soft, so that he can work it easy; and this he does by keeping it hot. But after he gets it finished, he heats it in the fire, and dips it in water, so as to cool it suddenly, and that makes it hard. But, if he left it so, it would be so hard that it would break all to pieces as soon as it was used. So he holds it again over the fire, and heats it a little, to

take out a part of the temper, and make it just of the hardness that he wishes. An instrument that is very hard is called *high-tempered*; one that is very soft is *low-tempered*. This is a good illustration of *temper* as it appears in us. A *high temper* is one that is easily excited, and that runs so high as to be in danger of doing great mischief. A *low temper* is a disposition easy and indifferent, like a knife tempered so little that the edge will turn the first time it is used. Now you want temper enough not to be indifferent, but not so much as to fly all in pieces. And I know nothing on which your usefulness and happiness more depend, than in the proper regulation of your temper; and not your own happiness alone, but the happiness of all around you. One of the first and greatest moral lessons is, to learn Prov. 16:32 to control your temper. "He that is slow to anger," says Solomon, "is better than the mighty; and he that ruleth his spirit, than he that Prov. 25:28 taketh a city." But, "He that hath no rule over his own spirit is like a city that is broken down and without walls." By indulging an ungoverned temper, you expose yourself to many evils. You show the weak points of your character, and lose the good opinion of others, and your own self-respect. You cannot help thinking meanly of yourself after having broken out in a sudden gust of anger, or given indulgence to a peevish, fretful spirit. To be ill-humored, peevish, or cross, is to be unhappy, and to make others unhappy. But a sweet temper will not only make you happy, but, like the balmy breezes of a summer evening, it will shed a sweet fragrance all around you. Nothing will render your character more unlovely than ill temper. Nor, if habitually indulged at home, can it be concealed even from the most careless observer. You will carry the mark of it wherever you go. There will be the ill-natured scowl, the knit brow, the distorted features, which no sweet-scented soap can wash out, and no cosmetic hide. It will spoil the most elegant features, and mar the most beautiful countenance. But a sweet temper will hide a thousand defects, and render the most ordinary features beautiful and lovely. I do not know anything that adds a greater charm to the youthful countenance. But, if you would have a sweet temper, you must suppress every ill-natured feeling; never suffer yourself to be angry at trifles, nor get into a storm of passion on any account: neither indulge a peevish, fretful disposition; but, on the contrary, cultivate and cherish *good nature*, in every possible way. Strive to be pleased with everything around you, unless it is positively bad; and never suffer the ill humors of others to disturb your own tranquillity. The noisy cataract comes splashing its muddy waters over the side of the mountain, leaping from rock to rock, now shouting, now murmuring, now scolding, now rushing on in the wildest fury, till it plunges into the great river; but the river rolls quietly on its majestic way, undisturbed by the babbling waterfall, which only makes a momentary ripple upon the surface of its placid waters. But, suppose the river should stop its course, to quarrel with the noisy waterfall, what would be the consequence? The whole country would be inundated with the fury of its pent-up waters. You cannot afford to get angry with everyone that is disposed to treat you ill. It costs too much. Did you ever see a dog barking at the moon? And what did the moon do? It went right straight on, and minded nothing about it. The moon can't afford to stop and quarrel with the dog that barks at it.

"I know it is very foolish to be angry," perhaps you will say; "but how can I help it? I am suddenly provoked, and fall into a passion before I have time to think of it." The best remedy I can recommend is, that you make it a rule never to be angry till you have had time to consider whether you have anything to be angry about. And, in making inquiry, do not ask whether the conduct that provoked you was bad; but, in the first place, try if you cannot find some apology for it, or some palliation; and, second, whether, admitting it to be as bad as it seems, it is really worth so great a sacrifice of feeling, on your part, as you will have to make, if you indulge your passions. And, among other considerations, ask yourself how this thing will appear a hundred years hence, when both yourself and the person who has provoked you, will be in eternity: "If I indulge my passions in this thing, shall I then be able to look back upon it with pleasure?" Some such reflections as these will tend greatly to cool your anger; and most likely, before you have thought upon the matter many minutes, you will conclude that it is not worth while to be angry.

So likewise, if you are given to fretfulness and ill humor, consider whether there is any sufficient cause why you should thus make yourself miserable? And you will probably find that all your trouble is imaginary. Remember that everything that concerns you is ordered by the providence of God; and think how much cause of thankfulness you have, every day, for his goodness. And what has he done that you should fret against him? He has perhaps suffered your will to be crossed; but he has done it for your good. Think, also, how this will appear a hundred years hence? "How will my fretfulness appear, when I look back upon it, from another world?" And if there were no sin in it, is there not much folly? – for "why should I make myself miserable?"

2. NEVER GIVE THE LEAST INDULGENCE TO A JEALOUS OR ENVIOUS SPIRIT. To be *jealous*, is to suspect others of being unfriendly to us, or of a design to injure us. To be *envious*, is to be displeased with the prosperity of others, especially if they are likely to excel us. The effect of these two passions upon the disposition

is very similar. If you are jealous of any person, you will be always looking for some evil design in his conduct; and your imagination will conjure up a thousand things that never had any existence, except in your own mind. This passion, habitually indulged, very often settles down into a kind of *monomania*, or partial insanity. I have known persons, whose imaginings, through the influence of jealousy, became realities to their minds, and they would roundly assert as facts, the things that they had imagined respecting others. Such persons are perpetually in trouble, because they fancy someone is plotting against them. Your own comfort, therefore, depends on your suppressing the first motions of this evil affection. While you should be on your guard against imposition, and never confide implicitly in strangers, nor put yourself in the power of anyone whose character has not been proved, yet you should presume others to be friendly till they show themselves otherwise, and always give their conduct the best construction it will bear.

Let me give you an example. There is Laura Williams – she is always in trouble, for fear someone does not like her. If any of her companions seem to take more notice of some other one than of herself, she begins to be jealous that their professions of friendship are not real; and if anyone happens not to notice her for once, she considers it a slight; and so her feelings are perpetually disturbed. She is never happy. Sometimes she will weep, as if her heart would break, for some fancied slight; when, in reality, she has no occasion for trouble, and might just as well laugh as cry. She will be unhappy as long as she lives, and perhaps crazy before she dies, if she does not overcome this passion.

Envy is a more depraved passion than *jealousy*; but the effect upon the character is nearly similar. You will find a melancholy illustration of the nature and effects of envy, in the story of Haman, in the Book of Esther. Though exalted to the second place in the kingdom, he could not enjoy his elevation, so long as Mordecai the Jew sat in the king's gate. He could endure no rival.

But you will find examples enough of this passion among your own companions. There are those that cannot bear a rival; and if any of their companions excel themselves, they hate them. But consider how mean and ignoble such a feeling is. A truly generous spirit will rejoice in whatever is excellent – will love excellence wherever it appears; but a mean and selfish spirit would monopolize everything to itself, and be offended, if excelled by others. Every noble sentiment revolts at the spirit of envy; so that this base passion always defeats itself. The envious person would be exalted above all; but envy debases him below all, and renders him despicable and miserable.

3. ACQUIRE THE HABIT OF REGARDING EVERYONE WITH FEELINGS OF GOODWILL. There are some persons, who accustom themselves to look upon others with a critical eye, and seem to take pleasure in detecting and exposing their failings. This leads to misanthropy; it makes people ill-natured. It leads them to look upon almost everyone as an object of aversion. If this disposition begins in early life, and continues to be cultivated, it will grow and increase, till it settles at last into a sour, morose, malignant temper, that can never look with pleasure or satisfaction upon any human being.

Instead of indulging such a temper, you should look with feelings of *goodwill* upon everyone. Do not regard others with a critical eye. If they are not incorrigibly bad, so as to render them dangerous associates, overlook their faults, and study to find out some redeeming qualities. Consider that they belong to the same great family – that they are as good by nature as yourself – that they have immortal souls, to be saved or lost. Try what excuses or apologies you can find for their faults in the circumstances in which they have been bred. And though you may not see fit to make choice of them as your friends, yet *feel kindly towards them*. But especially, do not forget that you are not faultless yourself. This will exert a softening influence upon your own character; and you will find yourself much more happy in studying the good qualities of others, and exercising feelings of charity and goodwill toward them, than you will in criticising and finding fault. The one course will make you amiable and happy – the other, unlovely and miserable.

4. GIVE FREE INDULGENCE TO EVERY NOBLE AND GENEROUS SENTIMENT. Rejoice when you see others prosperous. Why should you be unhappy, that another is more prosperous than yourself, if you are not injured by it? If you love your neighbor as yourself, his prosperity will be as grateful to you as your own. Rejoice, also, in the excellence of others. A truly noble heart loves excellence for excellence's sake. A generous heart is forgetful of self; and when it sees excellence, it is drawn toward it in love. It would scorn to put little self between it and a worthy object.

This disposition should also be carried out in action. A generous and noble spirit will not always be contending for its own rights. It will yield rather than contend. Contention, among companions and associates, for each other's rights, is a source of great unhappiness; and when it becomes habitual, as it sometimes does among brothers and sisters at home, it spoils the disposition. "That is *mine*," says one. "No," says the other, "it is not yours, it is mine." And without waiting quietly to look into the matter, and investigate the question of right, they fall into a sharp contention. The matter in question was a mere trifle. It was not worth the sacrifice of *good nature* which it cost. How much better both would feel, to keep good-natured, and give each other the reasons for their claims, and if they cannot agree, for one or the other to yield! Or, rather, how much more noble, if the contention be, which shall be allowed the privilege of yielding! There is more pleasure in one act of generosity than in all that can be enjoyed by selfish possession; and nothing will render you more lovely in the eyes of others than a noble and generous disposition.

5. BE GENTLE.   Gentleness is opposed to all severity and roughness of manners. It diffuses a mild, bland, amiable spirit through all the behavior. It has much to do with the cultivation of the affections. Where this is wanting, none of the amiable affections will flourish. A gentle spirit will show itself in a gentle behavior, and a gentle behavior will react upon the spirit, and promote the growth of all the mild and amiable affections. You can distinguish the gentle by the motion of the head, or the sound of their footsteps. Their movements are quiet and noiseless. There is a charm in their behavior which operates to secure for them the good opinion of all.

6. BE KIND.   Every kind act that is performed increases the kind feelings of the heart. If you treat your brothers and sisters kindly, you will feel more kindly toward them; while, if you treat them with harshness and severity, or ill-treat them in any manner, it will seal up your affections toward them, and you will be more inclined to treat them with coolness and indifference. If you are habitually kind to everyone, embracing every opportunity in your power to perform some office of kindness to others, you will find your good-will toward all increasing. You will be universally beloved, and ev-

eryone will be kind to you. See that little girl! She has run back to assist her little brother, who has lost his shoe in the mud. How kindly she speaks to him, to soothe his feelings and wipe his tears! Some sisters that I have seen would have been impatient of the delay, and scolded him in a cross and angry manner for the tumble he made. But with a heart full of sympathy, she forgets herself, and is intent only on helping him out of trouble, and quieting his grief. But she has hardly got under way again, before she meets a little girl, who has just fallen down and spilled her berries, crying over her loss. Without once thinking of the trouble it would give her, she speaks kindly to the little girl, helps her pick up the lost fruit, and then assists her to pick enough more to make up her loss. Every where she is just so, always glad of an opportunity to show kindness to everyone she meets. And she gets her pay as she goes along. The happiness she feels, in thus being able to contribute to the comfort of others, is far beyond anything she could receive from mere selfish enjoyment. And, in addition to this, she gets the goodwill of others, which makes them kind to her in return.

7. KEEP SELF OUT OF VIEW, AND SHOW AN INTEREST IN THE AFFAIRS OF OTHERS. This will not only interest others in you, but it will tend to stifle selfishness in your own heart, and to cultivate disinterested feeling. Sympathize with others; enter into their feelings; and endeavor, in heart and feeling, to make their interest your own; so that there may be a soil for disinterested feeling to grow in. If you see others enjoying themselves, rejoice with them. Make the case your own, and be glad that they have occasion to rejoice. "Rejoice with them that do rejoice." If you have truly benev- Rom. 12:15 olent feelings, it will certainly be an occasion of joy to you to see

them prosperous and happy, whoever they are. On the other hand, sympathize with misery and distress. "Weep with them that weep." Wherever you see misery, let it affect your heart. And never fail, if it is in your power, to offer relief. And, often, you can afford the best relief to those of your own age – your companions, but especially your inferiors – by showing that you are affected with their troubles, that you sympathize with them. Cultivate the habit of *feeling* for others. When you see or read of the sufferings of the poor, when you read of the condition of the heathen, who know not the way of salvation, let your sympathies flow forth toward them. Learn to feel for others' woe, and it will improve your own heart. But, besides this, you will find yourself rewarded with the affections of others.

Rom. 12:15

✌ Educating the heart

Thus I have given you a few brief hints, to show how the affections may be cultivated. I must leave you to apply them in practice to everyday life, and to carry out the principle, in its application to all the circumstances in which you may be placed; which principle is, as much as possible, to repress and refrain from exercising every bad feeling or affection, and to cherish and cultivate the good, bringing them into exercise on every fit occasion, that they may grow into habits.

You will see, by what I have said under the various heads of this chapter, that the idea of *educating the heart* is no mere *figure of speech*, but a reality, of great importance to your character and well-being through life. Your parents and teachers will, of course, pay attention to this matter; but they cannot succeed in it without your cooperation. And with you it must be an everyday work. You must carry it out in all your conduct and feelings, and seek the grace of God to aid you in so difficult a work. Without an *educated heart*, you will never make a GENTLEMAN. The fine feelings and good tempers which I have described are indispensable to *good breeding*. You cannot have polished manners with a *rough heart*. You may *put on* the gentleman; but it will appear out of place. You cannot change the nature of *pig*. You may wash him over and over again, and make him ever so clean; you may even dress him up in white linen garments – but he will immediately return to his wallowing in the mire.

❧ Educating the heart

Thus I have given you a few brief hints, to show how the affections may be cultivated. I must leave you to apply them in practice to everyday life, and to carry out the principle, in its application to all the circumstances in which you may be placed; which principle is, as much as possible, to repress and refrain from exercising every bad feeling or affection, and to cherish and cultivate the good, bringing them into exercise on every fit occasion, that they may grow into habits.

You will see, by what I have said under the various heads of this chapter, that the idea of *educating the heart* is no mere *figure of speech*, but a reality, of great importance to your character and well-being through life. Your parents and teachers will, of course, pay attention to this matter; but they cannot succeed in it without your cooperation. And with you it must be an everyday work. You must carry it out in all your conduct and feelings, and seek the grace of God to aid you in so difficult a work. Without an *educated heart*, you will never be fit to fill the station designed for a WOMAN. A woman's excellence and influence *lie in the heart*; and no outward accomplishments can compensate for the want of a *good heart*.

CHAPTER 15

EDUCATION OF THE MIND

Mental faculties

The term *Mind* is often employed to signify all the faculties of the soul. But I shall use it in application to the *intellectual faculties*, in distinction from the *moral*; as I have employed *heart* to denote the *moral*, in distinction from the *intellectual*. I shall not undertake to give a strictly philosophical distinction of the mental faculties, but shall comprehend them in the following division, which is sufficient for my purpose, to wit: *Perception, Reason* or *Understanding, Judgment, Memory*, and *Imagination*. PERCEPTION is the faculty that receives ideas into the mind; as, when you look at a tree, immediately the idea of a tree is impressed on the mind through the sense of sight; or, when you touch an object, the idea of that object is impressed on your mind through the sense of touch; or, you may receive the idea of a spirit, from the explanations which you hear or read.

The REASON or UNDERSTANDING, is the faculty that considers, analyzes, and compares ideas received into the mind, and forms conclusions concerning them. For example, suppose you had never seen a watch: one is presented to you, and as soon as your eye rests upon it, you form an idea respecting it. Perhaps this idea is no more than that it is a very curious object. But, immediately, your understanding is employed in *considering* what it is, the perceptive faculty still being occupied in further discoveries. From the fact that there is motion, you conclude there must be some *power* within it; for motion is not produced without power. Here is *consideration* and *conclusion*, which is a regular operation of reason. But, to make further discoveries, you open the watch, to examine its parts. This is *analyzing*. You examine all the parts that you can see, on removing the case. You still see *motion* – all the wheels moving in regular order; but the *cause* of the motion, the *power* that moves, is yet unseen. You perceive a chain wound around a wheel, and attached to another wheel, around which it is slowly winding itself; and this chain appears to regulate the whole movement. You conclude that the power must be in this last-named wheel. Here is a conclusion from analyzing, or examining the parts separately.

The JUDGMENT is the same as what is popularly styled *common sense*. It is that faculty which pronounces a decision, in view of all the information before the mind, in any given case. For example, if you wish to determine what school you will attend, you first obtain all the information you can respecting the different schools that claim your attention. You consider and compare the advantages of each; and you decide according to your impression of their comparative merits. The faculty which forms this decision is called the *judgment*. You will readily perceive how very important this faculty is; for a person may be very learned, and yet a very great *dunce* in everything of a practical nature, if he fails in judgment or common sense. His learning will be of very little use to him, because he has not sense to use it to advantage.

The MEMORY is the faculty which *retains* the knowledge that is received into the mind. It is a wonderful faculty. It may be compared to an immense closet, with a countless number and variety of shelves, drawers, and cells, in which articles are stored away for future use, only one of which can be examined by the proprietor at the same time, and yet so arranged that he knows just where to look for the article he wants. It is supposed that no impression, once made upon the memory, can be obliterated; and yet the impression may not be called up for years. It lies there, till some association of ideas brings it up again; the faculty not being able to present more than one object distinctly before the mind at the same instant.

The IMAGINATION is that faculty which forms pictures in the mind of real or unreal scenes. It is the faculty that you exercise in your fanciful plays, and when your mind runs forward to the time that you expect to be engaged in the busy scenes of life, and you picture to yourself pleasures and enjoyments in prospect. It is the faculty chiefly exercised by the poet and the writer of fiction.

Objects of education

You will, perhaps, be tired of this explanation; but it was necessary, in order to prepare the way for what I have to say on the *education of the mind*. From the definition of education already given, you will perceive that my ideas differ very much from those entertained by most young people. Ask a young person what he is going to school for, and he will answer, *"To learn."* And his idea of learning is, simply, to *acquire knowledge*. This, however, is but a small part of the object of education. And this idea often leads youth to judge that much of what they are required to study is of no value to them; because they think they shall have no use for the particular science they are studying, in practical life. The chief objects of mental education are, to cultivate and discipline the mind, and to store it with those great facts and principles which compose the elements of all knowledge. The studies to be pursued, then, are to be chosen with reference to these objects, and not merely for the purpose of making the mind a vast storehouse of knowledge. This may be done, and yet leave it a mere lumber room. For without the capacity to analyze, and turn it to account, all the knowledge in the world is but useless lumber. It is of great importance that young people should understand and appreciate this principle, because it is intimately connected with their success in acquiring a good education. To this end, it is necessary that they should cooperate with their parents and teachers. This they will never be ready to do, if they suppose the only object of study is, to acquire a knowledge of the particular branches they are set to learn; for they cannot see the use of them. But, understanding the design of education to be, to discipline the mind, and furnish it with the elements of knowledge, there is no science, no branch of learning, but what is useful for these objects; and the only question, where education cannot be liberal, is, What branches will best secure these ends?

Mental discipline

This understanding of the objects of education is also necessary, to stimulate the young to prosecute their studies in the most profitable manner. If their object were merely to acquire knowledge, the more aid they could get from their teachers the better, because they would thus obtain information the more rapidly. But the object being to discipline the mind, call forth its energies, and obtain a thorough knowledge of elementary principles, what is *studied out*, by the unaided efforts of the pupil, is worth a hundred times more than that which is communicated by an instructor. The very effort of the mind which is requisite to study out a sum in arithmetic, or a difficult sentence in language, is worth more than it costs, for the increased power which it imparts to the faculties so exercised. The principles involved in the case will, also, by this effort, be more deeply impressed upon the mind. Such efforts are also exceedingly valuable, for the confidence which they inspire in one's power of accomplishment. I do not mean to commend self-confidence in a bad sense. For anyone to be so confident of his own power as to think he can do things which he cannot, or to fancy himself qualified for stations which he is not able to fill, is foolish and vain. But, to know one's own ability to do, and have confidence in it, is indispensable to success in any undertaking. And this confidence is inspired by unaided efforts to overcome difficulties in the process of education. As an instance of this, I recollect, when a boy, of encountering a very difficult sum in arithmetic. After spending a considerable time on it, without success, I sought the aid of the school teacher, who failed to render me any assistance. I then applied to several other persons, none of whom could give me the desired information. Thus I was thrown back upon my own resources. I studied upon it several days without success. After worrying my head with it one evening, I retired to rest, and *dreamed* out the whole process. I do not suppose there was anything supernatural in my dream; but the sum was the absorbing subject of my thoughts, and when sleep had closed the senses, they still ran on the same subject. Rising in the morning with a clear head, and examining the question anew, it all opened up to my mind with perfect clearness; all difficulty vanished, and in a few moments the problem was solved. I can scarcely point to any single event, which has had more influence upon the whole course of my life than this. It gave me confidence in my ability to succeed in any reasonable undertaking. But for this confidence, I should never have thought of entering upon the most useful undertakings of my life. But for this, you would never have seen this book, nor any other of the numerous works which I have been enabled to furnish for the benefit of the young. I mention this circumstance here, for the purpose of encouraging you to *independent mental effort.* In prosecuting your studies, endeavor always, if possible, to overcome every difficulty without the aid of others. This practice, besides giving you the confidence of which I have spoken, will give you a much better knowledge of the branches you are pursuing, and enable you, as you advance, to proceed much more rapidly. Every difficulty you overcome, by your own unaided efforts, will make the next difficulty less. And though at first you will proceed more slowly, your habit of independent investigation will soon enable you to outstrip all those who are still held in the leading-strings of their teachers. A child will learn to walk much sooner by being let alone, than to be provided with a go-cart. Your studies, pursued in this manner, will be much more interesting; for you are interested in any study just in proportion to the effort of mind it costs you.

Symmetry of mind

The *perceptive faculty* is developed first of all. It begins to be exercised by the child before it can speak, or even understand language. *Reason* and *judgment* are more slow in their development, though they begin to be exercised at a very early period. *Memory* is exercised as soon as ideas are received into the mind. The *imagination*, in the natural course of things, is developed latest of all; but it is often forced out too early, like flowers in a hotbed, in which case it works great injury to the mind.

You will perceive the great importance of bringing out the several faculties of the mind in their due proportion. If the *memory* is chiefly cultivated, you will have a great amount of knowledge floating loosely in your mind, but it will be of very little use. But the proper cultivation of the memory is indispensable, in order to render your knowledge available. Nor will it do for you to adopt the notion that nothing is to be committed to the keeping of the memory which is not fully understood. The memory is a *servant*, which must consent to do some things without knowing the reason why. The *imagination* is the beautiful flower that crowns the top of the plant. But if forced out too early, or out of due proportion, it will cover the stalk with false blossoms, which, in a little time, will wither, and leave it dry and useless. The *perception, reason*, and *judgment*, require a long course of vigorous exercise and severe training, in order to lay a solid foundation of character.

~

I shall leave this subject here, without suggesting any particular means of cultivating the mind, leaving you to apply the principles here laid down to your ordinary studies. But in several subsequent chapters, I shall have some reference to what I have said here.

CHAPTER 16

READING

Importance of reading

Reading occupies a very important place in education. It is one of the principal means of treasuring up knowledge. It is, therefore, highly necessary that a taste for reading should be early cultivated. But a mere *taste for reading*, uncontrolled by intelligent principle, is a dangerous appetite. It may lead to ruinous consequences. The habit of reading *merely for amusement*, is a dangerous habit. *Reading for amusement* furnishes a constant temptation for reading what is injurious. It promotes, also, an *unprofitable manner* of reading. Reading in a hasty and cursory manner, without exercising your own thoughts upon what you read, induces a bad habit of mind. To profit by reading depends, not so much on the *quantity* which is read, as upon the *manner* in which it is read. You may read a great deal, in a gormandizing way, as the glutton consumes food, and yet be none the better, but the worse for what you read.

Danger of bad books

If you would profit by reading, you must, in the first place, be careful *what you read*. There are a multitude of books, pamphlets, periodicals, and newspapers, in circulation at the present day, which cannot be read, especially by the young, without great injury, both to the mind and heart. If anyone should propose to you to associate with men and women of the lowest and most abandoned character, you would shrink from the thought – you would be indignant at the proposition. But it is not the mere bodily presence of such characters that makes their society dangerous. It is the communion which you have with their minds and hearts, in their conduct and conversation. But a great portion of the popular literature of the day is written by such characters. By reading their writings, you come into communion with their minds and hearts, as much as if you were personally in their company. In their writings, the fancies which fill their corrupt minds, and the false and dangerous principles which dwell in their depraved hearts, are transferred to paper, to corrupt the unwary reader. Here are, likewise, glowing descriptions of evil conduct, more fascinating to the youthful heart than the example itself would be, because the mischief is artfully concealed behind the drapery of fine literary taste, and beautiful language. There are, likewise, many such writings, the productions of persons of *moral lives*, but of *corrupt principles*, which are equally dangerous. You would not associate with a person whom you knew to be an unprincipled character, even though he might be outwardly moral. He would be the more dangerous, because you would be less on your guard. If it is dangerous to keep company with persons of bad character or bad principles, it is much more so to keep company with bad books.

I have treated at large on the subject of *novel reading*, and other objectionable writings, in my *Young Lady's Guide*; and to that I must refer you, for my reasons, more at length, for condemning such reading. I shall here only suggest, for the regulation of your reading, a few simple rules.

1. ALWAYS HAVE SOME DEFINITE OBJECT IN VIEW, IN YOUR
READING.   While pursuing your education, you will be so severely taxed with hard study, that reading merely for diversion or amusement does not furnish the relaxation which you need. It keeps the
body idle and the mind still in exercise; whereas, the diversion
which you need, is something that will exercise the body and relax
the mind. If your object is diversion, then it is better to seek it in
useful labor, sprightly amusements, or healthful walks. I can think
of nothing more injurious to the young than spending the hours
in which they are released from study, bending over novels, or the
light literature of our trashy periodicals. Not only is the health seriously injured by such means, but the mind loses its vigor. The high
stimulus applied to the imagination creates a kind of mental intoxication, which renders study insipid and irksome. But reading is an
important part of education, and some time should be devoted to
it. Instead of mere amusement, however, there are higher objects
to be aimed at. These are, first, to store the mind with useful knowledge; second, to cultivate a correct taste; third, to make salutary
impressions upon the heart. For the first, you may read approved
works on all the various branches of knowledge; as history, biography, travels, science, and religious truth. For the second, you may
read such works of imagination and literary taste as are perfectly
free from objection, on the score of religion and morality – and
these but sparingly at your age; for the third, such practical works
of piety as you will find in the Sabbath school library. But, for all
these purposes, the *Bible* is the great Book of books. It contains history, biography, poetry, travels, and doctrinal and practical essays.
Any plan of reading will be essentially defective, which does not
contemplate the daily reading of the Bible. You ought to calculate
on reading it through, in course, every year of your life.

2. BE EXCEEDINGLY CAREFUL WHAT YOU READ.   Do not take
up a book, paper, or periodical, that happens to fall in your way,
because you have nothing else to read By so doing, you will expose yourself to great evils. But, though a book be not decidedly
objectionable, it may not be *worth reading.* There are so many good
books, at the present day, that it is not worth while to spend time
over what is of little value; and it is better to read the Bible alone,
than to spend time over a poor book. Avoid, especially, the ficti-
tious stories that you will find in newspapers and popular mag-
azines. They are generally the worst species of fiction, and tend
strongly to induce a vitiated taste, and an appetite for novel reading. If you once become accustomed to such reading, you will find
it produce a kind of *moral intoxication,* so that you will feel as uneasy without it, as the drunkard without his cups, or the smoker
without his pipe. It is much the safer way for young people to be
wholly directed by their parents (or their teachers, if away from
home) in the choice of their reading. Make it a rule never to read
any book, pamphlet, or periodical, till you have first ascertained
from your parents, teachers, or minister, that it is safe, and worth
reading.

3. THINK AS YOU READ.   Do not drink in the thoughts of others
as you drink water; but examine them, and see whether they carry
conviction to your own mind; and if they do, think them over, till
they become incorporated with your own thoughts, part and par-
cel of your own mind. Lay up facts and principles in your memory.
Let the beautiful thoughts and striking ideas that you discover be
treasured up as so many gems and precious stones, to enrich and
beautify your own mind. And let your heart be impressed and benefited by the practical thoughts you find addressed to it.

4. REDEEM TIME FOR READING.   Although it would be improper for you to take the time appropriated for study, or to rob yourself of needful diversion, yet you may, by careful economy, save some time every day for reading. A great deal of time is thrown away by the indulgence of dilatory habits, or consumed in a careless, sauntering vacancy. If you follow system, and have a time for everything, and endeavor to do everything with despatch, in its proper season, you will have time enough for everything that is necessary to be done.

CHAPTER 17

WRITING

Aversion to writing

Writing, or COMPOSING, is one of the best exercises of the mind. It is, however, I am sorry to say, an exercise to which young people generally show a great aversion. One reason, perhaps, is, that, to write well, requires *hard thinking*. But I am inclined to think the chief reason is, that the difficulties of writing are magnified. There is, also, a want of wisdom in the choice of subjects. Themes are frequently selected for first efforts, which require deep, abstract thinking; and the mind not being able to grasp them, there is a want of thought, which discourages new beginners. The first attempts should be made upon subjects that are easy and well understood; such as a well-studied portion of history, a well-known story, or a description of some familiar scene; the object being to clothe it in suitable language, and to make such reflections upon it as occur to the mind. Writing is but *thinking on paper*; and if you have any thoughts at all, you may commit them to writing.

Another fault in young beginners is, viewing composition as a *task* imposed on them by their teachers, and making it their chief object to cover a certain quantity of paper with writing; and so the sooner this task is discharged the better. But you must have a higher aim than this, or you will never be a good writer. Such efforts are positively injurious. They promote a careless, negligent habit of writing. One well-written composition, which costs days of hard study, is worth more, as a discipline of mind, than a hundred offhand, careless productions. Indeed, one good, successful effort will greatly diminish every succeeding effort, and make writing easy. You will do well, then, first to select your subject some time before you write, and think it over and study it, and have your ideas arranged in your mind before you begin. Then write with care, selecting the best expressions, and clothing your thoughts in the best dress. Then carefully and repeatedly read it over, and correct it, studying every sentence, weighing every expression, and making every possible improvement. Then lay it aside awhile, and afterwards copy it, with such improvements as occur at the time. Then lay it aside, and after some days revise it again, and see what further improvements and corrections you can make, and copy it a second time. If you repeat this process half a dozen times, it will be all the better. Nor will the time you spend upon it be lost. One such composition will conquer all the difficulties in the way of writing; and every time you repeat such an effort, you will find your mind expanding, and your thoughts multiplying, so that, very soon, writing will become an easy and delightful exercise; and you will, at length, be able to make the first draught so nearly perfect that it will not need copying. But you never will make a good writer by offhand, careless efforts.

Letter writing

Letter writing, however, is a very different affair. Its beauty consists in its simplicity, ease, and freedom from formality. The best rule that can be given for letter writing is, to imagine the person present whom you are addressing, and write just what you would say in conversation. All attempts at effort, in letter writing, are out of place. The detail of particulars, such as your correspondent would be interested to know, and the expression of your own feelings, are the great excellences of this kind of writing. Nothing disappoints a person more than to receive a letter full of fine sentiments, or didactic matter, such as he might find in books, while the very information which he desired is left out, and perhaps an apology at the close for not giving the news, because the sheet is full. In a letter, we want *information of the welfare of our friends*, together with the warm gush of feeling which fills their hearts. These are the true excellences of epistolary writing.

CHAPTER 18

INDOLENCE

There is no greater enemy to improvement than an indolent spirit. An aversion to effort paralyzes every noble desire, and defeats every attempt at advancement. If you are naturally indolent, you must put on resolution to overcome it, and strive against it with untiring vigilance. There is not a single point, in the process of education, at which this hydra-headed monster will not meet you. "The sloth- Prov. 22:13 ful man saith, There is a lion without, I shall be slain in the street." There is always a lion in the way, when slothful spirits are called upon to make any exertion. *"I can't,"* is the sovereign arbiter of their destiny. It prevents their attempting anything difficult or laborious. If required to write a composition, they *can't* think of anything to write about. The Latin lesson is difficult; this word they *can't* find; that sentence they *can't* read. The sums in arithmetic are *so hard,* they *can't* do them. And so this lion in the way defeats everything. But those who expect ever to be anything, must not suffer such a word as *can't* in their vocabulary.

It is the same with labor. The indolent dread all exertion. When requested to do anything, they have something else to do first which their indolence has left unfinished; or they have some other reason to give why they should not attempt it. But if nothing else will do, the sluggard's excuse, *"I can't,"* is always at hand. Were it not for the injury to them, it would be far more agreeable to do, oneself, what is desired of them, than to encounter the painful scowls that clothe the brow, when they think of making an effort. Solomon has de-

Prov. 26:15 scribed this disposition to the life: "The slothful man putteth his hand in his bosom: *it grieveth him to take it out again.*"

But indolence is a source of great misery. There are none so happy as those who are *always active.* I do not mean that they should give themselves no relaxation from severe effort. But relaxation does not suppose *idleness.* To sit and fold one's hands, and do nothing, serves no purpose. Change of employment is the best recreation. And from the idea of employment, I would not exclude active and healthful sports, provided they are kept within due bounds. But to sit idly staring at vacancy is intolerable. There is no enjoyment in it. It is a stagnation of body and mind. An indolent person is, to the active and industrious, what a stagnant pool is to the clear and beautiful lake. Employment contributes greatly to enjoyment. It invigorates the body, sharpens the intellect, and promotes cheerfulness of spirits; while indolence makes a torpid body, a vacant mind, and a peevish, discontented spirit.

Indolence is a great waste of existence. Suppose you live to the age of seventy years, and squander in idleness one hour a day, you will absolutely throw away about three years of your existence. And if we consider that this is taken from the waking hours of the day, it should be reckoned six years. Are you willing, by idleness, to shorten your life six years? Then take care of the moments. Never fritter away time in doing nothing. Whatever you do, whether study, work, or play, enter into it with spirit and energy; and never waste

Eccl. 9:10 your time in sauntering and doing nothing. "Whatsoever thy hand findeth to do, do it with thy might; for there is no work, nor device, nor knowledge, nor wisdom, in the grave, whither thou goest."

CHAPTER 19

ON DOING ONE THING AT A TIME

✏ Busy idleness

What is worth doing at all, is worth the undivided attention; but John can never be satisfied to do but one thing at a time. By attempting to read or play while dressing, he consumes double the time that is necessary. He reads at the table, and, in consequence, keeps the table waiting for him to finish his meal. He turns his work into play, and thus his work is slighted, and frequently left half done. When he goes to his lesson, his attention is arrested by something else before he has fairly commenced, and he stops to look or listen. Or perhaps he insensibly falls into a reverie, and is engaged in building "castles in the air," till something happens to call back his spirit from the fairy land. The consequence is, the lesson is acquired but imperfectly, while twice the needful time has been spent upon it. At the same time, nothing else is accomplished. This is what I call *busy idleness*.

✏ Busy idleness

What is worth doing at all is worth the undivided attention; but Julia can never be satisfied to do but one thing at a time. By attempting to read or to play while dressing, she consumes double the time that is necessary. She reads at the table, and, in consequence, keeps the table waiting for her to finish her meal. She will turn her work into play, and thus slight her work, and have it to do over again. By the time she gets fairly interested in her lesson, her attention is arrested by something else, and she stops to look or listen. Or she insensibly falls into a reverie, and is engaged in building aerial castles, till something happens to call back her spirit from the fairy world. This will perhaps be repeated a dozen times in the study of one lesson. The consequence is, the lesson is acquired but imperfectly, while twice the needful time has been spent upon it. At the same time, nothing else has been accomplished. This is what I call *busy idleness.*

~

The true way to accomplish the most, and to do it in the best manner, is to confine the attention strictly to the thing in hand, and to bend all the energies of the mind to that one object, aiming to do it in the best possible manner, in the least possible time. By adopting this principle, and acting upon it, you will be surprised to find how much more expeditiously you will accomplish what you undertake, and how much better it will be done. It is indispensable to success in any undertaking.

Closely connected with this subject, is the *systematic division of time.* Where there is no system, one duty will jostle another, and much time will be wasted in considering what to do next; all of which would be avoided, by having a regular routine of duties, one coming after the other in regular order, and so having a set time for each. This cannot be carried out perfectly, because there will every day be something to do that was not anticipated. But it may be so far pursued as to avoid confusion and waste or time.

CHAPTER 20

ON FINISHING WHAT IS BEGUN

&a James Scott

Beginning things and leaving them unfinished, exerts a bad influence in the formation of character. If it becomes a habit, it will
make you so fickle that no one will put confidence in you. There is
James Scott. If you go into his room, you will find his table strewed,
and his drawer filled, with compositions begun and not completed;
scraps of verses, but no poem finished; letters commenced, but
not completed. Or, if you go to his playhouse, you will find a ball
half wound; a kite half made; a boat begun; one runner of a sled;
one wheel of a wagon; and other things to match. He wants energy
and perseverance to finish what he begins; and thus he wastes his
time in frivolous pursuits. He is very ready to *begin*; but before he
has completed what is begun, he thinks of something else that he
wishes to do; or he grows weary of what he is upon. He lives to no
purpose, for he *completes* nothing; and he might as well *do nothing*,
as to *complete nothing*.

&o Jane Henderson

Beginning things and leaving them unfinished, exerts a bad influence in the formation of character. If it becomes a habit, it will

make you so fickle that no one will put confidence in you. There is Jane Henderson. If you go into her room, you will find her table strewed, and her drawers filled, with compositions begun and not completed; scraps of verses, but no poem finished; a dozen letters begun, but not one completed; bits of lace commenced, and laid aside; a dozen different squares of patchwork begun, but not one full square among them all. She wants energy and perseverance to finish what she begins; and thus she wastes her time in frivolous pursuits. She is very ready to *begin*; but before she has completed what is begun, she thinks of something else that she wishes to do; or she grows weary of what she is upon, and so leaves it, and tries something else. She lives to no purpose, for she *completes* nothing; and she might as well *do nothing*, as to *complete nothing*.

~

If you indulge this practice, it will grow upon you, till you will become weak, irresolute, fickle, and good for nothing. To avoid this, begin nothing that is not worth finishing, or that you have not good reason to think you will be able to finish. But when you have begun, resolutely persevere till you have finished. There is a strong temptation, with the young, to abandon an undertaking, because of the difficulties in the way; but, if you persevere, and conquer the difficulties you meet with, you will gain confidence in yourself, and the next time, perseverance in your undertakings will be more easy. You may, however, make a mistake, and begin what you cannot or ought not to perform; in which case, perseverance would only increase the evil.

CHAPTER 21

CHOICE OF SOCIETY, AND

FORMATION OF FRIENDSHIPS

Character is formed under a great variety of influences. Sometimes a very trifling circumstance gives direction to the whole course of one's life. And every incident that occurs, from day to day, is exerting a silent, gradual influence, in the formation of your character. Among these influences, none are more direct and powerful than that exerted upon us by the companions with whom we associate; for we insensibly fall into their habits. This is especially true in childhood and youth, when the character is plastic, like soft wax – easily impressed.

But we cannot avoid associating, to some extent, with those whose influence is injurious. It is necessary, then, for us to distinguish society into *general* and *particular*. General society is that with which we are *compelled to associate*. Particular society is that which we *choose for ourselves*. In school, and in all public places, you are under the necessity of associating somewhat with all. But those whom you meet, in such circumstances, you are not compelled to make intimate friends. You may be courteous and polite to all, wherever and whenever you meet them, and yet maintain such a prudent reserve, and cautious deportment, as not to be much exposed to contamination, if they should not prove suitable companions.

But everyone needs *intimate friends*; and it is necessary that these should be well chosen. A bad friend may prove your ruin. You should therefore be slow and cautious in the formation of intimacies and friendships. Do not be suddenly taken with anyone, and so enter into a hasty friendship; for you may be mistaken, and soon repent of it. There is much force in the old adage, "All is not gold that shines." A pleasing exterior often conceals a corrupt heart. Before you enter into close intimacies or friendships, study the characters of the persons whom you propose to choose for companions. Watch their behavior and conversation; and if you discover any bad habits indulged, or anything that indicates a want of principle, let them not become your companions. If you discover that they disregard any of the commandments of God, set them down as unsafe associates. They will not only be sure to lead you astray, but you can place no dependence upon their fidelity. If they will break one of God's commands, they will another; and you can put no confidence in them. But even where you discover no such thing, ask the opinion of your parents respecting them before you choose them as your friends. Yet, while you are in suspense about the matter, treat them courteously and kindly. But when you have determined to seek their friendship, do not impose your friendship on them against their will. Remember that they have the same right as yourself to the choice of their friends; and they may see some objection to the formation of a friendship with yourself. Be delicate, therefore, in your advances, and give them an opportunity to *come half way*. A friendship cautiously and slowly formed will be much more likely to last than one that is formed in haste. But let the number of your intimate and confidential friends be small. It is better to have a few select, choice, and warm friends, than to have a great number, less carefully chosen, whose attachment is less warm and ardent. But you must not refuse to associate at all with the mass of the society where you belong; especially, if you live in the country. You must meet them kindly and courteously, on all occasions where the society in general in which you move is called together. You must not affect exclusiveness, nor confine yourself to the company of your particular friends, at such times. But be careful that you do not expose yourself to evil influences.

You ought not, at present, to form any intimate friendships with the other sex. Such friendships, at your age, are dangerous; and if not productive of any serious present evils, they will probably be subjects of regret when you come to years of maturity; for attachments may be formed that your judgment will then disapprove.

CHAPTER 22

𝔉 BAD COMPANY AND

MISCHIEVOUSNESS

There are some boys, who carelessly go any where that they can find amusement, without regard to the character of their company. They not only associate indiscriminately in general society, where they are obliged to go, as at school; but they seek the company of bad boys, or permit themselves to be enticed into it, because it affords them some momentary enjoyment.

A bad boy is one who has a *bad disposition*, which has never been subdued; or one of corrupt principles and bad habits. A boy with a bad disposition will be rough, quarrelsome, malicious in his temper, fond of mischief, and rude and unmannerly in his general behavior. A boy of corrupt principles is one who will not scruple to break the commands of God, when they stand in the way of his own gratification. He acts from the mere selfish desire of present enjoyment. A boy of bad habits is one who is in the habit of disobeying his parents, breaking the Sabbath, using bad language, lying, stealing, gaming, drinking, or doing wanton mischief. Any of these habits shows a character thoroughly corrupt.

If you go into the company of persons that are sick with the measles, whooping cough, smallpox, or any contagious disorder, in a short time you will be taken with the same disease. The very atmosphere of the room where they stay is full of contagion, and you will draw it in with your breath. So, likewise, *moral diseases* are contagious. There is an atmosphere of moral contagion and death surrounding persons of vicious habits. "Evil communications cor- 1 Cor. 15:33 rupt good manners." The sight of evil deeds, or the hearing of bad language, hardens the heart, and diminishes the abhorrence of sin, which is felt by those to whom vice is not familiar. If you consent to go into bad company, you will soon find yourself falling into their habits. And if you keep company with bad boys, you will soon have the reputation of being a bad boy yourself.

Bad company will lead you into practices that will end in your ruin and disgrace. If you could read the history of those who have been sent to prison or otherwise punished for their crimes, you would be surprised to find how many of them were led, insensibly, into the evil courses which ended in their ruin, by frequenting bad company. I will give you a single example, which is only one among thousands that might be set before you, to show the dangerous influence of evil companions. There was a boy in Stockport (England), who went to the Sabbath school, and was esteemed a very good boy; so that he was appointed a teacher of one of the classes. But about this time his father died; and his mother, being poor, was obliged to send him to work in the factory. There he met with bad boys, who were addicted to evil practices. They gradually led him into their own evil courses, till, at length, he lost all the good impressions he had received in the Sabbath school. He began to drink, and drinking led him to committing petty thefts. He became so dissolute that his mother could do nothing with him. He was turned out of his employment, and obliged to enlist as a soldier. He was sent into Spain. There he indulged his evil courses, and supplied himself with the means of gratifying his evil desires, by plundering the inhabitants. At the close of the war, he returned home. Soon after landing, he and his evil companions began to break into people's houses and commit robberies. He was detected, tried, and condemned to death, at the age of twenty-one.

Let me especially caution you against indulging a mischievous disposition, or joining with others in any schemes of mischief. I know of nothing more likely to get you into serious difficulty, or to lead you into vicious habits and dissolute practices. A few years ago, a young man was hung, in one of our seaport towns, for piracy. He was one of the *bad boys* of whom I have been speaking. He had a bad disposition, which had never been subdued. At home, he was turbulent and unsubmissive; abroad, he was a ringleader in mischief; at school, he was disobedient to his teacher, and set himself to work to organize the boys to resist the authority of their teachers. At length, he went to sea; and there he carried out the same disposition. He headed the sailors against the authority of the captain. After he had been some time at sea, he persuaded the rest of the crew to set the captain and mate of the vessel upon the ocean in an open boat. They then took possession of the vessel, and turned pirates, robbing every vessel they could find. They were captured; and this young man was brought home, tried and condemned, and hung for his crime. This was the result of a turbulent and ungovernable boy giving up himself to be a ringleader in mischief.

Boys who go from the country to the city are very apt to be drawn into bad company. Cities abound with boys who are old in mischief and crime. They take great delight in leading astray the simple-hearted; and if boys from the country come within the reach of their influence, they are almost sure to be ruined. The

great number of boys found in the houses of correction and reformation, and in the city prisons, are so many beacons to warn the
unwary of the danger of shipwreck on the rocks and shoals of evil
company.

In conclusion, let me commend to you the wholesome warning
and advice of Solomon: "My son, if sinners entice thee, consent Prov. 1:10
thou not." "Enter not into the path of the wicked, and go not in Prov. 4:14–16
the way of evil men. Avoid it, pass not by it, turn from it, and pass
away. For they sleep not, except they have done mischief; and their
sleep is taken away, unless they cause some to fall."

CHAPTER 22

✑ ORNAMENTAL EDUCATION

Nature abounds with profusion of ornament. The trees of the forest are crowned with beauty. The flowers of the field are arrayed in the most gorgeous combination of beautiful colors, surpassing the imitation of man. The bowels of the earth enclose the richest gems; and even its dens and caverns are garnished with beautiful workmanship, far exceeding the highest achievements of art. The animate creation, also, displays the same love of beauty. The wild beasts are arrayed in the richest furs. The fowls of the air, and even the serpent that crawls on the earth, are adorned with a profusion of rich and beautiful colors. And man, the crowning work of the Creator, is adorned with symmetry of shape and beauty of features. But, above all, the mind itself has one entire faculty for ornament. The imagination is the flower of the mind, which crowns the intellectual tree with beauty and glory.

The voice of nature, therefore, forbids us to banish ornament from our systems of education. But equally does the same voice forbid us to make ornament the chief end of education. It is neither the *beginning* nor *end* of it. The rose does not grow on the root of the tree, nor does the plant, at its first growth, display its gorgeous colors. The trunk of the tree, the stem of the plant, the branches and the leaves, all precede the flower. Those are the *substantials*, this is the *ornament*. The former must be matured before the latter can appear. So, likewise, the substantial parts of education must take precedence of the ornamental. And the flower itself is not merely nor mainly for *beauty*; but it is *in order to fruit*. So the ornamental branches of education, in their proper places, are to be pursued with an eye to usefulness. However, the flower must be a long time budding before it blooms; and so may the ornamental branches of education be commenced and pursued a long time before they arrive at such perfection as to display their beauty, or discover their usefulness.

The solid branches, then, are to occupy the first place, and receive the chief attention. But the ornamental branches, at their proper time and in their proper places, are not to be neglected. Young people, however, are inclined to give them an undue importance, and disposed to pursue them to the neglect of that which is solid and substantial. David compared the daughters of Jerusalem to "cornerstones, polished after the similitude of a palace." But the _{Psalm 144:12} stones must be quarried and beaten out into the proper shape, before they can be *polished*. Polishing is the last work. This shows the place that is to be given to ornamental education. No one can receive an ornamental education merely. There must first be a solid superstructure; after which comes the polish. There are, however, some ornamental branches, which need to be pursued a long time, before they arrive at any degree of perfection. Such are music, drawing, and painting. They cultivate particular faculties; and this cultivation must necessarily be slow in its progress. Music, as a science, is perhaps as useful a discipline of mind as any other study. The cultivation of the voice and of the ear, is also of great importance. So, also, is the skillful use of the fingers, in playing on instruments; which is much more easily acquired in childhood than at any other period of life.

Drawing and painting cultivate the eye, and impart a quick perception of beauty. They also give the power of transferring to paper the image imprinted on the mind through the sense of sight. These branches are not merely ornamental, but often highly useful.

A good education is that process by which all the faculties and powers of the mind are developed in due proportion. That is a one-sided education which cultivates highly some particular faculties, while it neglects others. Such a mind will be deformed and out of proportion. To produce a well-balanced mind, the solid parts of education must receive the chief attention, because they constitute the very foundation of character. But it is a great mistake to conclude that they are all that is necessary, especially for females. By an exclusive attention to the solid branches, and that in a high degree, the character is rendered too masculine. There is need of the softening influence of those pursuits which are designed chiefly to embellish. And this should not be forgotten, in the pursuit of letters. The imagination and the taste should be cultivated, within proper bounds, so as to give symmetry of character.

Taste is, perhaps, not a distinct faculty by itself, but rather a combination of the faculties, concentrating them upon an object, and giving a nice and quick perception of beauty or deformity. It is exercised with respect to language, in discerning its correctness and beauty, or its incorrectness and deformity, without any process of reasoning or any comparison with rules of grammar or rhetoric. In a similar manner, it detects and points out, at a glance, the beauty or the deformity, the excellences or defects, of a picture or a landscape, or whatever object it beholds. This faculty, or combination of faculties, is cultivated by the study of music, drawing, painting, etc., with respect to the eye and ear; and in the study of language, with respect to the conceptions of the mind, and the manner of expressing them. I know of nothing, in the whole process of education, which contributes more to personal enjoyment than the cultivation of a correct taste. It also greatly recommends one to the regard of others. And, if chastened with piety, it may contribute to devotional feeling, by increasing our admiration of the beauties of creation, and through them leading us to adore the wisdom of the Creator.

CHAPTER 23

ON AMUSEMENTS

The human system is formed for alternate labor and rest, and not for incessant activity; and to provide for this, the night follows the day and the Sabbath the six days of labor. But not only is rest necessary after labor, but activity in a different direction. When you are carrying a burden of any kind, you find relief in a change of position. A poor boy was employed in turning a wheel, by which he was enabled to do something for his mother. A lady, observing him steadily employed at what appeared to be a very laborious occupation, inquired whether he did not get tired. He replied that he was often very tired. "And what do you do when you are tired?" she further inquired. "Oh," said he, "I take the other hand." He had learned that a change of position gave him rest. Neither the mind nor the body is capable of being incessantly exerted, in one direction, without injury. Like the bent bow, they will loses their elasticity. The body, after labor, and the mind, after study, need unbending, especially in youth, while the muscles of the body have not acquired maturity or solidity, and the powers of the mind are yet developing. At this period of life relaxation and amusement are especially necessary; and those young persons who eschew all play, and confine themselves to books and labor, must, in the natural course of things, suffer both in health and spirits. Healthful play is natural to the young, throughout the whole animal creation. The lamb, that emblem of innocence, is seen sporting in the fields, blithely bounding over the hills, as if desirous of expressing a grateful sense of its Creator's goodness. There is no more harm in the play of children than in the skipping of the lambs. It is necessary to restore the bent bow to its natural elasticity. It is the voice of nature, which cannot be hushed.

But having said so much, it is necessary to guard against improprieties and excesses in amusements. And yet, to determine what amusements are to be allowed, and what condemned, is no easy matter; for, while some kinds of amusement are evil in their own nature, and necessarily injurious, others are evil and injurious only on account of their *excess*, or of the *manner* in which they are pursued, or of the evils that are associated with them. My object is, not so much to point out what amusements are wrong, as to give you some rules by which you can judge for yourself.

I. Never engage in recreation at an *unsuitable time.* To neglect *duty* for the sake of amusement is not only wrong, but it will exert a bad influence upon your character. It tends to produce an immoderate love of amusement, and to break up all orderly and regular habits. Let your invariable rule be, "Business first, and then pleasure." Never suffer any kind of amusement to break in upon the time appropriated to labor or study.

II. Never do anything that is *disapproved by your parents or guardians.* They desire your happiness, and will not deprive you of any enjoyment, unless they see good reason for it. They may see evil where you would not perceive it. They regard your highest welfare. They look beyond the present, to see what influence these things will have on your character and happiness hereafter. They are also set over you of the Lord; and it is your duty not only to submit to their authority, but to reverence their counsel.

III. Engage in no amusement which is *disapproved by the most devoted and consistent Christians* of your acquaintance. I do not mean the few *cross* and *austere* persons, who always wear an aspect of gloom, and cannot bear to see the countenances of youth lighted up with the smile of innocent hilarity. But I mean those Christians who wear an aspect of devout cheerfulness, and maintain a holy and consistent life. Their judgment is formed under the influence of *devotional feeling*, and will not be likely to be far from what is just and right.

IV. Do nothing which you would be *afraid God should see*. There is no darkness nor secret place, where you can hide yourself from his all-searching eye. Contemplate the Lord Jesus Christ as walking by your side, as he truly is in spirit; and do nothing which you would be unwilling that he should witness, if he were with you in his bodily presence.

V. Do nothing the preparation for which *unfits you for religious duty*. If an amusement in which you are preparing to engage so takes up your mind as to interfere with your devotional exercises; if your thoughts run away from the Bible that you are reading to anticipated pleasures; or if those pleasures occupy your thoughts in prayer; you may be sure you are going too far.

VI. Engage in nothing *on which you cannot first ask God's blessing*. Do you desire to engage in anything in which you would not wish to be blessed and prospered? But God only can bless and prosper us in any undertaking. If, therefore, your feelings would be shocked to think of asking God's blessing on anything in which you would engage, it must be because your conscience tells you it is wrong.

VII. Engage in no amusement which *unfits you for devotional exercises.*   If, on returning from a scene of amusement, you feel no disposition to pray, you may be sure something is wrong. You had better not repeat the same again.

VIII. Engage in nothing which *tends to dissipate serious impressions.*   Seriousness, and a sense of eternal things, are perfectly consistent with serenity and cheerfulness. But thoughtless mirth, or habitual levity, will drive away such impressions. Whatever you find has this effect is dangerous to your soul.

IX. Reject such amusements as are generally *associated with evil.* If the influences which surround any practice are bad, you may justly conclude that it is unsafe, without stopping to inquire into the nature of the practice itself. Games of chance are associated with gambling and dissipation; therefore, I conclude that they cannot be safely pursued, even for amusement. Dancing, also, is associated with balls, with late hours, high and unnatural excitement, and dissipation; it is therefore unsafe. You may know the character of any amusement by the company in which it is found.

X. Engage in nothing which necessarily *leads you into temptation.* You pray every day (or ought to), "lead us not into temptation." But _{Matt. 6:13} you cannot offer up this prayer sincerely, and then run needlessly in the way of temptation. And if you throw yourself in the way of it, you have no reason to expect that God will deliver you from it.

XI. If you engage in any recreation, and return from it with a *wounded conscience*, set it down as evil.   A clear conscience is too valuable to be bartered for a few moments of pleasure; and if you find your conscience accusing you for having engaged in any amusement, never repeat the experiment.

XII.   Practise no amusement which *offends your sense of propriety*. A delicate sense of propriety, in regard to outward deportment, is in manners what conscience is in morals, and taste in language. It is not anything that we arrive at by a process of reasoning, but what the mind as it were instinctively perceives. It resembles the sense of taste; and by it one will notice any deviation from what is proper, before he has time to consider wherein the impropriety consists. There is a beauty and harmony in what is proper and right, which instantly strikes the mind with pleasure. There is a fitness of things, and an adaptation of one thing to another, in one's deportment, that strikes the beholder with sensations of pleasure, like those experienced on beholding the harmonious and beautiful blending of the seven colors of the rainbow. But when *propriety* is disregarded, the impression is similar to what we might suppose would be produced, if the colors of the rainbow crossed each other at irregular angles, now blending together in one, and now separating entirely, producing irregularity and confusion. The sensation produced upon the eye would be unpleasant, if not insufferable. Among the amusements which come under this rule are the vulgar plays that abound in low company, especially such as require the payment of forfeits, to be imposed by the victor. In such cases, you know not to what mortification you may be subjected. *Frolics*, in general, come under this head, where rude and boisterous plays are practised, and often to a late hour of the night, when all sense of propriety and even of courtesy is often forgotten.

XIII. Engage in nothing of *doubtful propriety*. The apostle Paul teaches that it is wrong to do anything the propriety of which we doubt; because, by doing that which we are not fully persuaded is right, we violate our conscience. It is always best to keep on the safe side. If you were walking near the crater of a volcano, you would not venture on ground where there was any danger of breaking through, and falling into the burning lake. You would keep on the ground where it was safe and sure. And so we should do, in regard to all questions of right and wrong. *Never venture where the ground trembles under your feet.*

XIV. Do nothing which you will *remember with regret on your dying bed.* It is well always to keep death in view; it has a good effect upon our minds. The deathbed always brings with it pains and sorrows enough. It is a sad thing to make work for repentance at such an hour. That is an honest hour. Then we shall view things in their true light. Ask yourself, then, before entering into any scene of amusement, how it will appear to you when you come to look back upon it from your dying bed.

XV. Do nothing in the midst of which you would be *afraid to meet death.* When preparing for a scene of pleasure, how do you know but you may be cut down in the midst of it? Sudden death is so common that it is folly to be in any place or condition in which we are not prepared to meet it. Many persons have been cut down in the midst of scenes of gaiety, and the same may occur again. A man in Germany was sitting at the gaming table. His card won a thousand ducats. The dealer handed over the money, and inquired how he would continue the game. The man made no reply. He was examined, and found to be a corpse! Similar scenes have occurred in the ballroom. In the midst of the merry dance, persons have been called suddenly out of time into eternity. A gentleman and lady started in a sleigh, to ride some distance to a ball, in a cold winter's night. Some time before reaching the place, the lady was observed to be silent. On driving up, the gentleman called to her, but no answer was returned. A light was procured, and he discovered, to his amazement, that he had been riding with a corpse! At no moment of life are we exempt from sudden death. He who holds us in his hand has a thousand ways of extinguishing our life in a moment. He can withhold the breath which he gave; he can stop the vital pulsation instantly; or he can break one of the thousand parts of the intricate machinery of which our mortal bodies are composed. No skill can provide against it. We ought not, therefore, to trust ourselves, for a single moment, in any place or condition where we are unwilling to meet death.

XVI. Do nothing for which you will be *afraid to answer at the bar of God.*   There every secret thing will be revealed. What was done in the darkness will be judged in open day. "Rejoice, O young man, in thy youth; and let thy heart cheer thee in the days of thy youth; and walk in the ways of thine heart, and in the sight of thine eyes: but know thou that for all these things God will bring thee into judgment." A young man, on leaving home to enter the army, was supplied with a small Bible, which, though a thoughtless youth, he always carried in his pocket. On one occasion, after a battle, he

Eccl. 11:9

took out his Bible, and observed that there was a bullet hole in the cover. His first impulse was, to turn over the leaves, and read the verse on which the ball rested. It was the passage just quoted. It brought before his mind all the scenes of mirth and sinful pleasure in which he had been engaged, and pressed upon him the fearful truth, that for all of them he was to be brought into judgment. It was the means of awakening him to a sense of his condition, and led to a change of heart and life. And why should not the same solemn impression rest upon your mind, with respect to all scenes of pleasure, and lead you carefully to avoid whatever you would not willingly meet at that awful tribunal?

~

If you apply these tests to the various amusements that are in vogue among young people, you may readily discern what you can safely pursue, and what you must sternly reject. It will lead you, especially, to detect the evils of all theatrical performances, balls, cards, and dancing parties, country frolics, and all things of a like nature. But it will not deprive you of one innocent enjoyment. A girl, ten or twelve years old, made a visit to a companion about her own age. Both of them were hopefully pious. On returning home, she told her mother she was sure Jane was a Christian. "Why do you think so, my daughter?" inquired the mother "Oh," said the daughter, *"she plays like a Christian."* In her diversions she carried out Christian principles, and manifested a Christian temper. This is the true secret of innocent recreation; and it cuts off all kinds of amusement that cannot be pursued in a Christian-like manner.

CHAPTER 24

GOVERNMENT OF THE TONGUE

The apostle James says, the *tongue* is an unruly member, and that it is easier to control a horse or a ship, or even to tame wild beasts and serpents, than to govern the tongue. And, though a very little member, it is capable of doing immense mischief. He even likens it to a fire. A very small spark, thrown into a heap of dry shavings, in a wooden house, in a great city, will make a terrible fire. It may burn up the whole city. So a very few words, carelessly spoken by an ungoverned tongue, may set a whole neighborhood on fire. You cannot, therefore, be too careful how you employ your tongue. It is of the highest importance to your character and usefulness, that you early acquire the habit of controlling this unruly member. For the purpose of aiding you in this, I shall give a few simple rules.

RULES FOR GOVERNING THE TONGUE

I. *Think before you speak.* Many persons open their mouths, and set their tongues a-going like the clapper of a windmill, as though the object was, to see how many words could be uttered in a given time, without any regard to their *quality* – whether *sense* or *nonsense*, whether good, bad, or indifferent. A tongue, trained up in this way, will never be governed, and must become a source of great mischief. But accustom yourself, before you speak, to consider whether what you are going to say is worth speaking, or whether it can do any mischief. If you cultivate this habit, your mind will speedily acquire an activity, that will enable you to make this consideration without waiting so long before answering your companions as to be observed; and it will impose a salutary restraint upon your loquacity; for you will find others often taking the lead of conversation instead of yourself, by seizing upon the pause that is made by your consideration. This will be an advantage to you, in two ways. It will give you something better to say, and will diminish the *quantity*. You will soon perceive that, though you say less than some of your companions, your words have more weight.

II. *Never allow yourself to talk nonsense.* The habit of careless, nonsensical talking, is greatly averse to the government of the tongue. It accustoms it to speak at random, without regard to consequences. It often leads to the utterance of what is not strictly true, and thus insensibly diminishes the regard for truth. It hardens the heart, and cherishes a trifling, careless spirit. Moreover, if you indulge this habit, your conversation will soon become silly and insipid.

III. *Do not allow yourself in the habit of JOKING with your companions.* This tends to cultivate severe sarcasm, which is a bad habit of the tongue. And, if you indulge it, your strokes will be too keen for your companions to bear; and you will lose their friendship.

IV. *Always speak the truth.* There is no evil habit, which the tongue can acquire, more wicked and mischievous than that of speaking falsehood. It is in itself very wicked; but it is not more wicked than mischievous. If all were liars, there could be no happiness; because all confidence would be destroyed, and no one would trust another. It is very offensive to God, who is a *God of truth*, and who has declared that all liars shall have their part in the lake that burns with fire and brimstone. It is a great affront and injury to the person that is deceived by it. Many young persons think nothing of deceiving their companions, in sport; but they will find that the habit of speaking what is not true, even in sport, besides being intrinsically wrong, will so accustom them to the utterance of falsehood, that they will soon lose that dread of a lie which used to fortify them against it. The habit of exaggeration, too, is a great enemy to truth. Where this is indulged, the practice of uttering falsehood, without thought or consideration, will steal on insensibly. It is necessary, therefore, in detailing circumstances, to state them accurately, precisely as they occurred, in order to cultivate the habit of truth-telling. Be very particular on this head. Do not allow yourself so little an inaccuracy, even, as to say you laid a book on the table, when you put it on the mantel, or on the window seat. In relating a story, it is not necessary that you should state every minute particular, but that what you do state should be exactly and circumstantially true. If you acquire this habit of accuracy, it will not only guard you against the indulgence of falsehood, but it will raise your character for truth. When people come to learn that they can depend upon the critical accuracy of whatever you say, it will greatly increase their confidence in you. But if you grow up with the habit of speaking falsehood, there will be very little hope of your reformation, as long as you live. The character that has acquired an habitual disregard of truth is most thoroughly vitiated. This one habit, if indulged and cherished, and carried with you from childhood to youth, and from youth upwards, will prove your ruin.

V. Remember that *all truth is not to be spoken at all times.*   The habit of uttering all that you know, at random, without regard to times and circumstances, is productive of great mischief. If you accustom your tongue to this habit, it will lead you into great difficulties. There are many of our own thoughts, and many facts that come to our knowledge, that prudence would require us to keep in our own bosom, because the utterance of them would do mischief.

VI. *Never, if you can possibly avoid it, speak anything to the disadvantage of another.*   The claims of justice or friendship may sometimes require you to speak what you know against others. You may be called to testify against their evil conduct in school, or before a court of justice; or you may be called to warn a friend against an evil or designing person. But, where no such motive exists, it is far better to leave them to the judgment of others and of God, and say nothing against them yourself.

VII. *Keep your tongue from talebearing.*   There is much said in the Scriptures against tattling. "Thou shalt not go up and down as a talebearer, among the children of thy people." "A talebearer revealeth secrets." "Where no wood is, the fire goeth out; and where there is no talebearer, the strife ceaseth." Young people are apt to imbibe a taste for neighborhood gossip, and to delight in possessing family secrets, and in repeating personal matters, neighborhood scandal, etc. But the habit is a bad one. It depraves the taste

Lev. 19:16

Prov. 11:13

Prov. 26:20

and vitiates the character, and often is the means of forming for life the vicious habit of talebearing. And talebearers, besides the great mischief they do, are always despised, as mean, mischievous, and contemptible characters.

~

If you will attentively observe and follow the foregoing rules, you will acquire such a habit of governing the tongue, that it will be an easy matter; and it will give dignity and value to your character, and make you beloved and esteemed, as worthy the confidence of all.

CHAPTER 25

ON THE ART OF AGREEABLE

& PROFITABLE CONVERSATION

There is, perhaps, no accomplishment which will add so much to your character and influence, as the art of conversing agreeably and well. To do this, however, requires a cultivated mind, richly stored with a variety of useful information; a good taste; a delicate sense of propriety; a good use of language; and an easy and fluent expression.

The most of these requisites can be acquired; and the rest, if naturally deficient, can be greatly improved. An easy, fluent expression is sometimes a natural talent; but, when not joined with a good understanding and a cultivated mind, it degenerates into mere loquacity. But, in order to be prepared to converse well, you must not only have your mind *well stored*, but its contents, if I may so speak, *well arranged*; so that you can at any time call forth its resources, upon any subject, when they are needed.

One of the principal difficulties, in the way of conversing well, is a hesitancy of speech – a difficulty of expressing one's ideas with ease and grace. This may arise from various causes. It may proceed from affectation – a desire to speak in fine, showy style. This will invariably defeat its object. You can never appear, in the eyes of

intelligent and well-bred people, to be what you are not. The more
simple and unaffected your style is, provided it be pure and chaste,
the better you will appear. Affectation will only make you ridiculous. But the same difficulty may arise from diffidence, which leads
to embarrassment; and embarrassment clouds the memory, and
produces confusion of mind and hesitancy of speech. This must be
overcome by degrees, by cultivating self-possession, and frequenting good society. The same difficulty may, likewise, arise from the
want of a sufficient command of language to express one's ideas
with ease and fluency. This is to be obtained by writing; by reading the most pure and classic authors, such as Addison's *Specta-
tor*; and by observing the conversation of well-educated people.
In order to have a good supply of well-chosen words at ready command, Mr. Whelpley recommends selecting from a dictionary several hundred words, such as are in most common use, and required
especially in ordinary conversation, writing them down, and committing them to memory, so as to have them as familiar as the
letters of the alphabet. A professional gentleman informs me, that
he has overcome this difficulty by reading a well-written story till
it becomes trite and uninteresting, and then frequently reading it
aloud, without any regard to the story, but only to the language, in
order to accustom the organs of speech to an easy flow of words. I
have no doubt that such experiments as these would be successful
in giving a freedom and ease of expression, which is often greatly
impeded for want of just the word that is needed at a given time.

There is no species of information but may be available to improve and enrich the conversation, and make it interesting to the
various classes of people. As an example of this, a clergyman re-
cently informed me that a rich man, who is engaged extensively
in the iron business, but who is very irreligious, put up with him
for the night. The minister, knowing the character of his guest, di-

rected his conversation to those subjects in which he supposed him to be chiefly interested. He exhibited specimens of iron ore, of which he possessed a variety; explained their different qualities; spoke of the various modes of manufacturing it; explained the process of manufacturing steel, etc.; interspersing his conversation with occasional serious reflections on the wisdom and goodness of God, in providing so abundantly the metals most necessary for the common purposes of life, and thus leading the man's mind "from Nature up to Nature's God." The man entered readily into the conversation, appeared deeply interested, and afterwards expressed his great admiration of the minister. The man was prejudiced against ministers. This conversation may so far remove his prejudices as to open his ear to the truth. But all this the minister was enabled to do, by acquainting himself with a branch of knowledge which many would suppose to be of no use to a minister. By conversing freely with all sorts of people upon that which chiefly interests them, you may not only secure their goodwill, but greatly increase you own stock of knowledge. There is no one so ignorant but he may, in this way, add something to your general information; and you may improve the opportunity it gives to impart useful information, without seeming to do it.

RULES FOR CONVERSATION

I. Avoid *affectation.*   Instead of making you appear to better advantage, it will only expose you to ridicule.

II. Avoid *low expressions.*   There is a dialect peculiar to low people, which you cannot imitate without appearing as if you were yourself low-bred.

III. Avoid *provincialisms*.   There are certain expressions peculiar
to particular sections of the country. For example, in New England, many people are in the habit of interlarding their conversation with the phrase, *"You see."* In Pennsylvania and New York,
the same use is made of *"You know."* And in the West and South,
phrases peculiar to those sections of the country are still more
common and ludicrous. Avoid all these expressions, and strive after a pure, chaste and simple style.

IV. Avoid all *ungrammatical* expressions.

V. Avoid *unmeaning exclamations*, as, "Oh my!" "Oh mercy!" etc.

VI. Never speak unless you have *something to say*.   "A word fitly
spoken is like apples of gold in pictures of silver."

Prov. 25:11

VII. Avoid *prolixity*.   Make your language concise and perspicu-
ous, and strive not to prolong your speech beyond what is necessary, remembering that others wish to speak as well as yourself. Be
sparing of anecdote; and only resort to it when you have a good illustration of some subject before the company, or when you have
a piece of information of general interest. To tell a story well, is a
great art. To be tedious and prolix in storytelling, is insufferable.
To avoid this, do not attempt to relate every minute particular; but
seize upon the grand points. Take the following specimen of the
relation of the same incident by two different persons: "You see,
I got up this morning, and dressed myself, and came downstairs,
and opened the front door; and oh, if it didn't look beautiful! For,
you see, the sun shone on the dew – the dew, you know, that hangs
in great drops on the grass in the morning. Well, as the sun shone
on the dewdrops, it was all sparkling, like so many diamonds; and

it looked so inviting, you see, I thought I must have a walk. So, you see, I went out into the street, and got over the fence – the fence, you know, the back side of the barn. Well, I got over it, and walked into the grove, and there I heard the blue jay, and cock-robin, and ever so many pretty birds, singing so sweetly. I went along the foot-path to a place where there is a stump – the great stump, you know, James, by the side of the path. Well, there – Oh, my! – what should I see, but a gray squirrel running up a tree!"

How much better the following: "Early this morning, just as the sun was peeping over the hill, and the green grass was all over sparkling with diamonds, as the sun shone upon the dewdrops, I had a delightful walk in the grove, listening to the sweet music of the birds, and watching the motions of a beautiful gray squirrel, running up a tree, and hopping nimbly from branch to branch." Here is the story, better told, in less than half the words.

Never specify any particulars which would readily be understood without. In the relation of this incident, all the circumstances detailed in the first specimen, previous to entering the grove, are superfluous; for if you were in the grove early in the morning, you could not get there without getting out of your bed, dressing yourself, opening the door, going into the street, and getting over the fence. The moment you speak of being in the grove early in the morning, the mind of the hearer supplies all these preliminaries; and your specifying them only excites his impatience to get at the point of your story. Be careful, also, that you never relate the same anecdote the second time to the same company; neither set up a laugh at your own story.

VIII. Never interrupt others while they are speaking. Quietly wait till they have finished what they have to say, before you reply. To interrupt others in conversation is very unmannerly.

IX. You will sometimes meet with very talkative persons, who are not disposed to give you a fair chance. *Let them talk on.* They will be better pleased, and you will save your words and your feelings.

X. Avoid, as much as possible, *speaking of yourself.* When we meet a person who is always saying *I*, telling what he has done, and how he does things, the impression it gives us of him is unpleasant. We say, "He thinks he knows everything, and can teach everybody. He is great in his own eyes. He thinks more of himself than of everybody else." True politeness leads us to keep ourselves out of view, and show an interest in other people's affairs.

XI. Endeavor to make your conversation *useful.* Introduce some subject which will be profitable to the company you are in. You feel dissatisfied when you retire from company where nothing useful has been said. But there is no amusement more interesting, to a sensible person, than intelligent conversation upon elevated subjects. It leaves a happy impression upon the mind. You can retire from it, and lay your head upon your pillow with a quiet conscience.

CHAPTER 26

INQUISITIVENESS

The inhabitants of New England have the reputation of being inquisitive to a fault; and perhaps with some justice. This disposition grows out of a good trait of character, carried to an extreme. It comes from a desire after knowledge. But this desire becomes excessive, when exercised with reference to matters which it does not concern us to know. When it leads us to pry into the concerns of others, from a mere vain curiosity, it becomes a vice. There are some people who can never be satisfied, till they *see the inside of everything*. They must know the why and the wherefore of everything they meet with. I have heard an amusing anecdote of this sort. There was a man who had lost his nose. A *Yankee*, seeing him, desired to know how so strange a thing had happened. After enduring his importunity for some time, the man declared he would tell him, if he would promise to ask him no more questions; to which the other agreed. "Well," said the man, *"it was bit off."* "Ah," replied the Yankee, *"I wish I knew who bit it off!"* This is a fair specimen of the morbid appetite created by excessive inquisitiveness.

When inquisitiveness goes no farther than a strong desire to obtain useful information, and to inquire into the reason of things, or when it desires information concerning the affairs of others from benevolent sympathy, then it is a valuable trait of character.

But when the object is to gratify an idle curiosity, it is annoying to others, and often leads the person who indulges it into serious difficulty. And the more it is indulged, the more it craves. If you gratify this disposition till it grows into a habit, you will find it very difficult to control. You will never be able to let anything alone. You will want to look into every drawer in the house; to open every bundle that you see, and never be satisfied till you have seen the inside of everything. This will lead you into temptation. It can hardly be supposed that one who is so anxious to *see* everything should have no desire to *possess* the things that are seen. Thus, what began in curiosity may end in coveting and thieving. But if it does not lead you so far astray as this, it will bring you into serious difficulty with your parents, or your friends whose guest you are; for they will not be satisfied to have their drawers tumbled, packages opened, and every nice article fingered. This disposition, too, will lead you to inquire into the secrets of your friends; and this will furnish a temptation to tattling. What you have been at such pains to obtain, you will find it difficult to keep to yourself. You will want to share the rare enjoyment with others. And when the story comes round to your friend or companion, whose confidence you have betrayed, you will, to your great chagrin and mortification, be discarded. A delicate sense of propriety will lead you to avoid prying too closely into the affairs of others. You will never do it from mere curiosity. But if any of your friends so far make you a confidant as to lead you to suppose that they need your sympathy or aid, you may, in a delicate manner, inquire farther, in order to ascertain what aid you can render. You may, also, make some general inquiries of strangers, in order to show an interest in their affairs. But beyond this, you cannot safely indulge this disposition.

CHAPTER 27

ON THE IMPORTANCE OF

BEING ABLE TO SAY NO

It often requires great courage to say NO. But by being able promptly, on occasion, to utter this little monosyllable, you may save yourself a deal of trouble. If mother Eve had known how to say *no*, she might have saved herself and her posterity from ruin. And many of her children, who have lost their character and their all, might have been saved, if they had only had courage promptly to say NO. Your safety and happiness depend upon it.

You are importuned by some of your companions to engage in some amusement, or to go on some excursion, which you know to be wrong. You resolutely and promptly say NO, at the outset, and there is the end of it. But if you hesitate, you will be urged and importuned, until you will probably yield; and having thus given up your own judgment, and violated your conscience, you will lose your power of resistance, and yield to every enticement.

✌ Joseph and Reuben

Joseph has cultivated decision of character. He never hesitates a moment when anything wrong is proposed. He rejects it instantly.

The consequence is, his companions never think of going to him, when they have any mischievous scheme on foot. His prompt and decisive NO they do not wish to encounter. His parents can trust him any where, because they have no fears of his being led astray. And this relieves them of a load of anxiety.

Reuben is the opposite of this. He wishes to please everybody, and therefore has not courage to say *no* to any. He seems wholly unable to resist temptation. He is, therefore, always getting into difficulty – always doing something that he ought not, or going to some improper place, or engaging in some improper diversions, through the enticement of his companions. His parents scarcely dare trust him out of their sight, they are so fearful that he will be led astray. He is thus a source of great anxiety to them, and all because he cannot say NO.

✌ Jane and Mary

Jane has cultivated decision of character. She never hesitates a moment when anything wrong is proposed. She rejects it instantly. The consequence is, her companions never think of coming to her with any proposal of an exceptionable nature. Her prompt and decisive NO they do not desire to encounter. Her parents can trust her any where, because they have no fears of her being led astray. And this relieves them of a load of anxiety.

But Mary is the opposite of this. She wishes to please everybody, and therefore has not courage to say *no* to any. She seems to have no power to resist temptation. Hence, she is always getting into difficulty – always doing something that she ought not, or going to some improper place, or engaging in some improper diversions, through the enticement of her companions. Her parents scarcely dare trust her out of their sight, they are so fearful that she will be led astray. She is a source of great anxiety to them; and all because she cannot say NO.

～

Now, let me beg of you to learn to say NO. If you find any difficulty in uttering it – if your tongue won't do its office, or if you find a *"frog in your throat,"* which obstructs your utterance – go by yourself, and practise *saying* no, NO, NO! till you can articulate clearly, distinctly, and without hesitation; and have it always ready on your tongue's end, to utter with emphasis to every girl or boy, man or woman, or evil spirit, that presumes to propose to you to do anything that is wrong. Only be careful to say it respectfully and courteously, with the usual *prefixes* and *suffixes*, which properly belong to the persons to whom you are speaking.

CHAPTER 28

ON BEING USEFUL

Can you find anything, in all the works of Nature, which is not made for some use? The cow gives milk, the ox labors in the field, the sheep furnishes wool for clothing, and all of them provide us with meat. The horse and the dog are the servants of man. Every animal – every little insect – has its place, and its work to perform, carrying out the great design of its Creator. And so it is with the inanimate creation. The earth yields its products for the use of man and beast; and the sun, and the air, and the clouds (each in turn) help forward the work. And to how many thousand uses do we put the noble, stately tree! It furnishes houses for us to live in, furniture for our convenience, fuel to make us warm, ships to sail in, and to bring us the productions of other lands. It yields us fruit for food, and to gratify our taste. And so you may go through all the variety of animal and vegetable life, and you will find everything designed for some use. And, though there may be some things of the use of which you are ignorant, yet you will find everything made with such evidence of design, that you cannot help thinking it must have been intended for some use.

Now, if everything in creation is designed for some use, surely you ought not to think of being useless, or of living for nothing. God made you to be useful; and, to answer the end of your being, you must begin early to learn to be useful. "But how can I be useful?" you may ask. "I wish to be useful. I am anxious to be qualified to fill some useful station in life – to be a missionary or a teacher, or in some other way to do good. But I do not see what good I can do now." Though you may not say this in so many words, yet I have no doubt that such thoughts may often have passed through your mind. Many people long to be useful, as they suppose, but think they must be in some other situation, to afford them the opportunity. This is a great mistake. God, who made all creatures, has put everyone in the right place. In the place where God has put you, there you may find some useful thing to do. Do you ask me what useful thing you can do? You may find a hundred opportunities for doing good, and being useful, every day, if you watch for them. You can be useful in assisting your mother; you can be useful in helping your brothers and sisters; you can be useful in school, by supporting the authority of your teacher, and by being kind and helpful to your playmates. If you make it the great aim of your life to be useful, you will never lack opportunities.

I have seen young persons, who would take great delight in mere play or amusement; but the moment they were directed to do anything useful, they would be displeased. Now, I do not object to amusement, in its proper place; for a suitable degree of amusement is useful to the health. But pleasure alone is a small object to live for; and if you attempt to live only to be amused, you will soon run the whole round of pleasure, and become tired of it all. But if you make it your great object to be useful, and seek your chief pleasure therein, you will engage in occasional amusement with a double relish. No one can be happy who is not useful. Pleasure soon satiates. One amusement soon *grows gray*, and another is sought; till, at length, they all become tasteless and insipid.

Let it be your object, then, every day of your life, to be useful to yourself and others. In the morning, ask yourself, "What useful things can I do today? What can I do that will be a lasting benefit to myself? How can I make myself useful in the family? What can I do for my father or mother? What for my brothers or sisters? And what disinterested act can I perform for the benefit of those who have no claim upon me?" Thus you will cultivate useful habits and benevolent feelings. And you will find a rich return into your own bosom. By making yourself useful to everybody, you will find everyone making a return of your kindness. You will secure their friendship and good will, as well as their bounty. You will find it, then, both for your interest and happiness to BE USEFUL.

CHAPTER 29

ON BEING CONTENTED

The true secret of happiness is, to be contented. "Godliness," says the apostle Paul, "*with contentment*, is great gain." These two are *great gain*, because, without them, all the gain in the world will not make us happy. Young people are apt to think, if they had this thing or that, or if they were in such and such circumstances, different from their own, they would be happy. Sometimes they think, if their parents were only rich, they should enjoy themselves. But rich people are often more anxious to increase their riches than poor people are to be rich; and the more their artificial wants are gratified, the more they, are increased. "The eye is not satisfied with seeing, nor the ear filled with hearing." Solomon was a great king, so rich that he was able to get whatever his heart desired. He built great palaces for himself; he filled them with servants; he treasured up gold and silver; he bought gardens, and vineyards, and fields; he bought herds of cattle, with horses and carriages; he kept men and women singers, and players on all sorts of instruments; whatever his eyes desired he kept not from them; he withheld not his heart from any joy; but with it all he was not satisfied. He called it all "vanity and vexation of spirit." So you may set your heart at rest, that riches will not make you happy. Nor would you be any more happy, if you could exchange places with some other persons, who seem to you to have many more means of enjoyment than yourself. With these things that dazzle your eyes, they have also their trials; and if you take their place, you must take the bitter with the sweet.

But young people sometimes think, if they were only men and women, and could manage for themselves, and have none to control them, then they would certainly be happy, for they could do as they please. But in this they are greatly mistaken. There will then be a great increase of care and labor; and they will find it more difficult to *do as they please* than they do now. If they have none to control them, they will have none to provide for them. True, they may then manage for themselves; but they will also have to support themselves. Those who have lived the longest, generally consider youth the happiest period of life, because it is comparatively free from trouble and care, and there is more time for pleasure and amusement.

But there is one lesson, which, if you will learn it in youth, will make you happy all your days. It is the lesson which Paul had learned. You know that he suffered great hardships in traveling on foot, in various countries, to preach the gospel. He was often persecuted, reviled, defamed, beaten, and imprisoned. Yet he says, Phil. 4:11 *"I have learned in whatsoever state I am, therewith to be content."* There are several things which should teach us this lesson. In the first place, God, in his holy providence, has placed us in the condition where we are. He knows what is best for us, and what will best serve the end for which he made us; and of all other situations, he has chosen for us the one that we now occupy. Who could choose so well as he? And then, what can we gain by fretting about it, and worrying ourselves for what we cannot help? We only make ourselves unhappy. Moreover, it is very ungrateful and wicked to complain of our lot, since God has given us more and better than we deserve. It is better to look about us, and see how many things we have to be thankful for; to look upon *what we have*, rather than *what we have not*. This does not, indeed, forbid our seeking to improve our condition, provided we do it with submission to the will of God. We ought to use all fair and lawful means to this end; but not in such a spirit of discontent and repining, as will make us miserable if we are disappointed. If you desire to be happy, then, BE CONTENTED.

CHAPTER 30

UNION OF SERIOUS PIETY
WITH HABITUAL CHEERFULNESS

It is a mistake often made by young people, to associate religion with a downcast look, a sad countenance, and an aching heart. Perhaps the mistakes of some good people, in putting on a grave and severe aspect, approaching even to moroseness, may have given some occasion for this sentiment. I do not know, indeed, how prevalent the sentiment is among the young. I can hardly think it is common with those who are religiously educated. As for myself, I well remember that, in my childhood, I thought true Christians must be the happiest people in the world. There is no doubt, however, that many pleasure-loving young people do look upon religion with that peculiar kind of dread which they feel of the presence of a grave, severe maiden aunt, which would spoil all their pleasure. And, I do not deny, that there are certain kinds of pleasure which religion spoils; but then it first removes the taste and desire for them, after which the spoliation is nothing to be lamented. It is true, also, that there are some things in religion which are painful. Repentance for sin is a painful exercise; self-denial is painful; the resistance of temptation is sometimes trying; and the subduing of evil dispositions is a difficult work. But, to endure whatever of suffering there is in these things, is a saving in the end. It is less painful than the tortures of a guilty conscience, the gnawings of remorse, and the fear of hell. It is easier to be endured than the consequences of neglecting religion. If you get a sliver in your finger, it is easier to bear the pain of having it removed, than it is to carry it about with you. If you have a decayed tooth, it is easier to have it extracted than to bear the toothache. So it is easier to repent of sin than to bear remorse and fear. And the labor of resisting temptation, and of restraining and subduing evil dispositions, is not so great an interference with one's happiness as it is to carry about a guilty conscience.

There is, however, nothing in true piety inconsistent with habitual cheerfulness. There is a difference between cheerfulness and levity. Cheerfulness is serene and peaceful. Levity is light and trifling. The former promotes evenness of temper and equanimity of enjoyment; the latter drowns sorrow and pain for a short time, only to have it return again with redoubled power.

The Christian hope, and the promises and consolations of God's word, furnish the only true ground of cheerfulness. Who should be cheerful and happy, if not one who is delivered from the terrors of hell and the fear of death – who is raised to the dignity of a child of God – who has the hope of eternal life – the prospect of dwelling forever in the presence of God, in the society of the blessed, and in the enjoyment of perfect felicity? But no one would associate these things with that peculiar kind of mirth, which is the delight of the pleasure-loving world. Your sense of propriety recoils from the idea of associating things of such high import with rudeness, frolicking, and mirth. Yet there is an innocent gaiety of spirits, arising from natural vivacity, especially in the period of childhood and youth, the indulgence of which, within proper bounds, religion does not forbid.

There is a happy medium between a settled, severe gravity and gloom, and frivolity, levity, and mirth, which young Christians should strive to cultivate. If you give unbounded license to a mirthful spirit, and indulge freely in all manner of levity, frivolity, and foolish jesting, you cannot maintain that devout state of heart which is essential to true piety. On the other hand, if you studiously repress the natural vivacity of youthful feeling, and cultivate a romantic kind of melancholy, or a severe gravity, you will destroy the elasticity of your spirits, injure your health, and very likely become peevish and irritable, and of a sour, morose temper; and this will be quite as injurious to true religious feeling as the other. The true medium is, to unite serious piety with habitual cheerfulness. Always bring Christian motives to bear upon your feelings. The gospel of Jesus Christ has a remedy for everything in life that is calculated to make us gloomy and sad. It offers the pardon of sin to the penitent and believing, the aid of grace to those that struggle against an evil disposition, and succor and help against temptation. It promises to relieve the believer from fear, and afford consolation in affliction. There is no reason why a true Christian should not be cheerful. There are, indeed, many things, which he sees, within and without, that must give him pain. But there is that in his Christian hope, and in the considerations brought to his mind from the Word of God, which is able to bear him high above them all.

Let me, then, earnestly recommend you to cultivate a serious but cheerful piety. Let your religion be neither of that spurious kind which expends itself in sighs, and tears, and gloomy feelings, nor that which makes you insensible to all feeling. But while you are alive to your own sins and imperfections, exercising godly sorrow for them, and while you feel a deep and earnest sympathy for

those who have no interest in Christ, let your faith in the aton-
ing blood of Jesus, and your confidence in God, avail to keep you
from sinking into melancholy and gloom, and make you cheerful
and happy, while you rest in God.

~

And now, gentle reader, after this long conversation, I must take
leave of you, commending you to God, with the prayer that my
book may be useful to you, in the formation of a well-balanced
Christian character; and that, after you and I shall have done the
errand for which the Lord sent us into the world, we may meet in
heaven. GOD BLESS YOU!

Typeset
using X∃LATEX
in 12-point Minion
with headings in Beorcana

ℰ

www.ingramcontent.com/pod-product-compliance
Lightning Source LLC
Chambersburg PA
CBHW021052090426
42738CB00006B/305